Collins Primary Maths
Pupil Book 2

6

Series Editor: Peter Clarke

Authors: Andrew Edmondson, Elizabeth Jurgensen,
Jeanette Mumford, Sandra Roberts

Contents

	To check that the sum of the angles of a triangle is 180°: for example by measuring or paper folding To calculate angles in a triangle or around a point	54–55
Measures: (area and perimeter)	To calculate the area of a shape formed from rectangles, including using a calculator with memory	56–57
	To calculate the area of a shape formed from rectangles, including using a calculator with memory	58–59, 60–61
	To use, read and write standard metric units of mass (kg, g), including their abbreviations, and relationships between them	62–63
Measures: (mass)/Making decisions	To convert smaller units to larger units (e.g. g to kg), and vice versa To know imperial units (lb, oz) To know rough equivalents of lb and kg and oz and g	64–65 66–67
Problems involving measures (mass)	To identify and use appropriate operations (including combinations of operations) to solve word problems involving numbers and quantities based on measures (mass), using one or more steps	68–69
Handling data	To solve a problem by representing and interpreting data in tables, charts, graphs and diagrams, including those generated by a computer, for example: line graphs (e.g. for a multiplication table, a graph, pairs of numbers adding to 8)	70–71
	To solve a problem by representing and interpreting data in tables, charts, graphs and diagrams, including those generated by a computer, for example: line graph, where intermediate points may have meaning (e.g. for distance/time)	72–73, 74–75
Mental calculation strategies (+)/Pencil and paper procedures (+)	To extend written methods to column addition of numbers involving decimals	76–77, 78–79
Mental calculation strategies (–)/Pencil and paper procedures (–)	To extend written methods to column subtraction of numbers involving decimals	80–81
Mental calculation strategies (+ and –)	To consolidate all strategies from previous year, including: derive quickly decimals that total 0·1; derive sums and differences	84–85
	To use known number facts and place value to consolidate mental addition/subtraction: add or subtract four-digit multiples of 100/find what to add to a decimal with units, tenths and hundredths to make the next higher whole number or tenth; add or subtract a pair of decimal fractions each less than 1 and with up to two places	86–87, 86–89
Checking results of calculations	To check with the inverse operation when using a calculator	90–91
Properties of numbers and number sequences	To make general statements about odd or even numbers, including the outcome of products	96–97
	To find simple common multiples To know and apply simple tests of divisibility	98–99 100–101, 102–103
	To recognise prime numbers to at least 20 To factorise numbers to 100 into prime factors	104–105

Changing places

Practice

1 What is the place value of the red digits?

a 2 695 411   b 9 154 367   c 4 259 413

d 2 587 499   e 3 621 847   f 1 087 964

g 7 538 429   h 6 333 847   i 8 920 473

2 Now choose two of the numbers and write them out in words.

3 Copy and complete the following table into your book.
Round the numbers to the nearest multiple of 10, 100 and 1000.

Number	Multiple of 10	Multiple of 100	Multiple of 1000
27 862			
96 785			
14 538			
19 003			
75 499			
50 273			
83 251			
31 628			
59 725			
91 351			

4 Multiply and divide each of these numbers by
10 up to a seven-digit number and down to
a number with three decimal places.

a 8   b 25   c 84

d 176   e 205   f 382

Example

$$6 \qquad\qquad 6$$
$$6 \times 10 = 60 \qquad 6 \div 10 = 0.6$$
$$600 \qquad\qquad 0.06$$
$$6000 \qquad\qquad 0.006$$
$$60\ 000$$
$$600\ 000$$
$$6\ 000\ 000$$

Refresher

1 What is the place value of the red digits?

   a 26 000   b 75 693   c 12 478   d 59 347   e 40 687

   f 36 527   g 64 283   h 77 912   i 62 834   j 99 458

2 Now choose two of the numbers and write them out in words.

3 Copy the following table into your book. Round the numbers to the nearest multiple of 10, 100 and 1000.

Number	Multiple of 10	Multiple of 100	Multiple of 1000
4687	4690	4700	5 000

   a 2951   b 5486   c 2177   d 4876   e 3501

   f 8752   g 1297   h 3868   i 9277   J 6534

4 Choose a number from each set and make up five calculations that involve multiplying by 10 or 100, and five calculations that involve dividing by 10 or 100.

Example
$91 \times 100 = 9100$

91	4	23
126	54 8 19	
15	6	41

400	9100	150
230	0·8 1900	12·6
60	410	5400

Challenge

Work out the missing numbers.

a $0.8 \times \boxed{} = 8$

b $56 \times \boxed{} = 56\ 000$

c $18 \div \boxed{} = 0.018$

d $72\ 000 \div \boxed{} = 72$

e $7.3 \times \boxed{} = 730$

f $148 \div \boxed{} = 0.148$

g $128 \times \boxed{} = 12\ 800$

h $\boxed{} \div 100 = 3.72$

i $\boxed{} \times 1000 = 470\ 000$

j $7\ 852\ 621 \div \boxed{} = 7852.621$

Negative differences

Practice

1 Write out these numbers. Write a number that can come between each one.

Example

−78 │−74│ −62 │−53│ −49 │−37│ −31 │−28│ −24

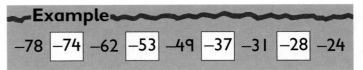

a −45 ☐ −41 ☐ −21 ☐ −12 ☐ 0

b −74 ☐ −66 ☐ −52 ☐ −34 ☐ −23

c −97 ☐ −92 ☐ −88 ☐ −70 ☐ −67

d −102 ☐ −52 ☐ −11 ☐ −1 ☐ 9

e −251 ☐ −167 ☐ −83 ☐ 0 ☐ 51

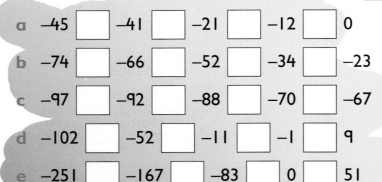

2 Find the difference between the numbers. Write an addition and a subtraction calculation to work out each one.

Example

3, −9

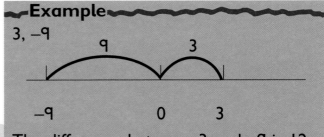

−9 0 3

The difference between 3 and −9 is 12.

a 4, −6   b 8, −1

c 3, −7   d −10, 5

e −7, 2   f 9, −7

g 12, −14   h −5, −16

i −1, −11   j −17, 8   k 15, −19   l 14, −20

m −18, −6   n 18, −7   o −19, 0   p 9, −15

Refresher

1 Order the following numbers from smallest to largest.
   a 0, –5, –7, 15, –23, 2
   b –12, –16, 12, 25, 0, 7
   c 62, –21, –4, 32, –32, –23
   d 37, –73, 5, –11, 0, 99
   e –26, –46, 36, 6, 16, –16

2 Find the difference between these numbers. Use the number line to help you.

–10 –9 –8 –7 –6 –5 –4 –3 –2 –1 0 1 2 3 4 5 6 7 8 9 10

   a 2, –3   b –4, 5   c –7, 1   d 9, –3   e 5, –6
   f 7, –1   g 0, –8   h 2, –10   i 10, –8   j –9, –6

Challenge

Work out these calculations without using a number line.

   a 2 – 51   b 35 – 47   c 12 – 59   d 75 – 126   e 89 – 99
   f –45 + 18   g –56 + 78   h –14 + 89   i –63 + 159   j –37 + 96
   k –154 + 84   l –68 + 15   m –167 + 77   n –267 + 148   o –208 + 163

Find the difference

Practice

In speech bubble:
−4, 7
I can check if the difference is 11 by doing −4 + 11 on the calculator.

1 Work out the difference between the two numbers. Then check your answer on a calculator. Write down the calculation you carry out on the calculator.

a −9, 15 b 12, −7 c −14, −3 d 11, −14 e 20, −1

f −18, 16 g 20, −13 h −19, −4 i 8, −8 j −18, −1

2 Work out these calculations on the calculator.
Write an inverse calculation and use it to check your answer.

~Example~
7 − 11 = −4
−4 + 11 = 7

a 9 − 12 b 6 − 15 c 8 − 13 d 10 − 18 e 4 − 18

f 17 − 25 g 9 − 20 h 7 − 16 i 3 − 24 j 2 − 28

k −14 + 5 l −33 + 25 m −18 + 20 n −19 + 11 o −10 + 15

p −6 + 18 q −16 + 19 r −3 + 24 s −5 + 27 t −21 + 33

Refresher

First work out the difference between the
two numbers, then complete the calculation
underneath and find the missing number.
Now work out this calculation on a calculator
to check your answer.

−2, 4
I can check my
answer, 6, by
doing −2 + 6 on
the calculator.

a −5, 6
−5 + ☐ = 6

b −8, 2
−8 + ☐ = 2

c −3, 7
−3 + ☐ = 7

d −6, 5
−6 + ☐ = 5

e −1, 9
−1 + ☐ = 9

f −2, 3
−2 + ☐ = 3

g −4, 8
−4 + ☐ = 8

h −9, 6
−9 + ☐ = 6

i −10, 5
−10 + ☐ = 5

j −3, 10
−3 + ☐ = 10

k −2, 5
−2 + ☐ = 5

l −8, 6
−8 + ☐ = 6

Challenge

1 I am thinking of a number. If I add 5 to it then subtract 12,
   I end up with negative 6. What was my number?

I am thinking …

2 I am thinking of a number. If I double it then subtract 16,
   I end up with negative 12. What was my number?

3 I am thinking of a number. If I add 3 then subtract 24,
   I end up with negative 18. What was my number?

4 Now make up a "think of a number" problem for your friend.

Time for times tables

Practice

Class 6 worked out how many different answers they could get from the number sentence.

$$3 + 7 \times 5 + 6 = \boxed{}$$

$3 + (7 \times 5) + 6 = 3 + 35 + 6 = 44$

$(3 + 7) \times 5 + 6 = 10 \times 5 + 6 = 56$

$3 + 7 \times (5 + 6) = 3 + 77 = 80$

$(3 + 7) \times (5 \times 6) = 10 \times 30 = 300$

1 How many different answers can you get from these calculations? (You can put brackets around any calculation – remember to calculate what is inside the brackets first!)

a $4 + 8 \times 7 + 6$ b $9 \times 7 + 4 + 6$

c $7 \times 12 \div 4 + 8$ d $56 \div 4 \times 2 \times 7$

e $8 + 12 \times 5 \div 4$ f $64 \div 8 \times 4 \times 3$

g $6 \times 6 \times 2 + 12$ h $100 \div 5 \times 5 + 4$

i $48 \div 8 \times 2 + 9$ j $8 + 9 \times 7 + 2$

2 Find up to four different ways to split these calculations using factors.

Circle the expanded calculation you find easiest to calculate, then write the answer to the calculation.

Example

$\boxed{16 \times 12}$ $\boxed{90 \div 6}$

$16 \times 6 \times 2$ $(90 \div 3) \div 2$

$16 \times 3 \times 4$ $(90 \div 2) \div 3$

$12 \times 4 \times 4$ $(30 \div 6) + (30 \div 6) + (30 \div 6)$

$12 \times 8 \times 2$

a 18×25 b 33×15

c 28×12 d $800 \div 16$

e 24×25 f $420 \div 12$

g $390 \div 15$ h 27×14

i $98 \div 14$ j 25×16

Refresher

Find the factors of these numbers.

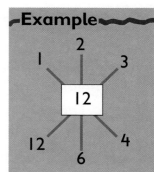

a 15

b 24

c 16

d 32

e 42

f 36

g 20

h 54

i 48

j 64

k 40

l 100

Challenge

1 Use brackets to make each answer an even number.

a $13 \times 4 \times 2 - 20$

b $4 \times 9 - 7 + 4$

c $30 \div 6 + 5 \times 3$

d $7 \times 7 + 9 \times 3$

e $6 \times 7 + 3 + 6$

f $56 - 24 \div 8$

g $48 + 15 \div 3 + 7$

h $56 \div 8 + 6$

i $47 - 11 \times 12 \div 3$

j $6 \times 6 \div 4 + 5$

2 Use brackets to make answers totalling 100.

a $4 \times 11 + 8 + 7$

b $40 - 15 \times 24 \div 6$

c $13 + 7 \times 14 - 9$

d $56 \div 2 + 8 \times 9$

e $8 \times 8 + 9 \times 4$

f $26 + 24 \times 16 \div 8$

g $85 + 23 - 32 \div 4$

h $14 + 6 \times 9 + 32$

i $5 \times 12 \times 4 - 28$

j $28 \times 2 - 21 \times 4$

Decimal halves

Practice

Each function machine halves numbers. The yellow machine halves each number once. The blue machine halves each number twice. Write the numbers that come out of each machine.

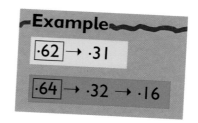

1
  a ·46
  b ·72
  c ·68
  d ·34
  e ·90
  f ·52

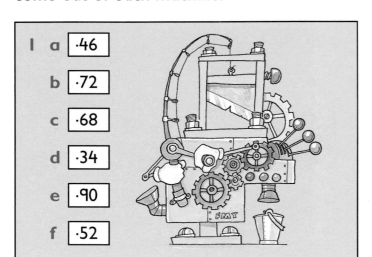

2
  a ·92
  b ·8
  c ·56
  d ·78
  e ·32
  f ·84

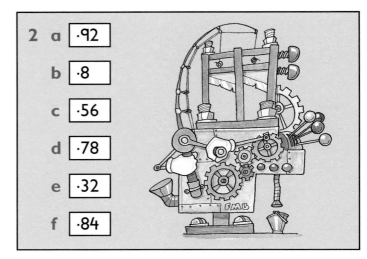

3
  a 12·8
  b 62·4
  c 48·4
  d 46
  e 32·24
  f 82

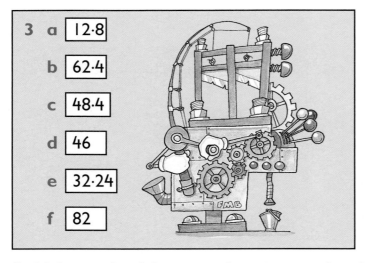

4
  a 15·6
  b 72·4
  c 26·3
  d 44·5
  e 27·8
  f 68·7

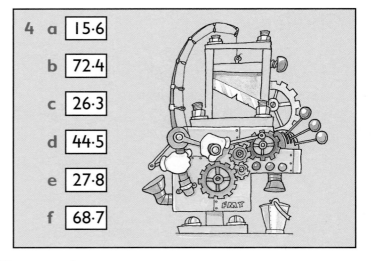

5   Halve each of these numbers in your head. Draw a diagram to show your answer. Check your answer is correct by performing the inverse operation. Complete the diagram.

  a 24·5   b 36·3   c 18·24
  d 16·7   e 28·9   f 42·1
  g 38·4   h 62·92   i 78·56

Example

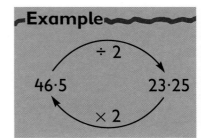

46·5 →(÷ 2)→ 23·25
23·25 →(× 2)→ 46·5

Refresher

Find the even numbers. Halve each even number.
Record your answer as a number sentence.

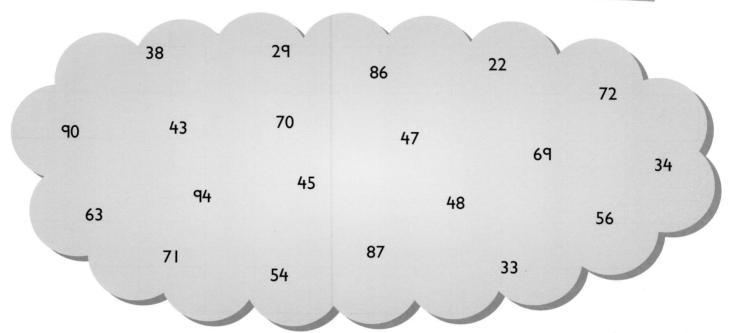

38   29   86   22
72
90   43   70   47
69   34
45
94   48   56
63
71   87
54   33

Challenge

Halving game

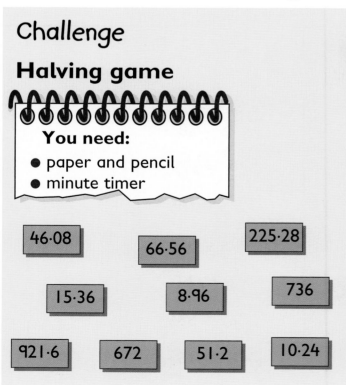

You need:
- paper and pencil
- minute timer

46·08   225·28
66·56
15·36   8·96   736
921·6   672   51·2   10·24

What to do

Play with a partner

1 Play in pairs and take turns to choose one of the numbers.

2 Both players write the number down.

3 Start the minute timer.

4 Halve the number and keep halving until the minute is up.

5 Compare your answers.

6 The person with the most correct numbers scores 1 point.

7 The first person to score 5 points is the winner.

In your head

Practice

1 Copy each grid. Fill in the answers on the grid by multiplying the numbers in the horizontal line by the number in the circle, and multiplying the numbers in the vertical line by the number in the square.

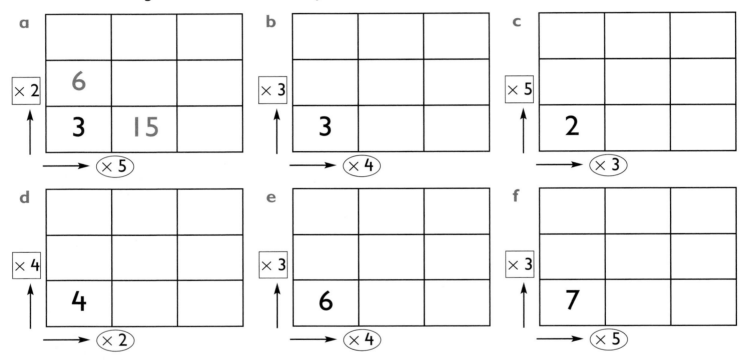

2 Find the missing number by multiplying mentally.

a 56 × ☐ = 336

b 37 × ☐ = 333

c 29 × ☐ = 203

d 84 × ☐ = 672

e 46 × ☐ = 276

f 72 × ☐ = 576

g 63 × ☐ = 441

h ☐ × 95 = 38

i ☐ × 4 = 312

j ☐ × 39 = 185

k ☐ × 74 = 666

l ☐ × 3 = 279

m ☐ × 67 = 536

n ☐ × 8 = 616

Refresher

Partition each of these calculations to find the answer.

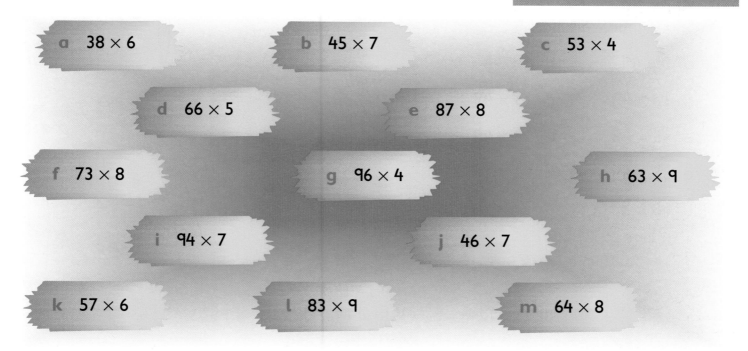

a   38 × 6

b   45 × 7

c   53 × 4

d   66 × 5

e   87 × 8

f   73 × 8

g   96 × 4

h   63 × 9

i   94 × 7

j   46 × 7

k   57 × 6

l   83 × 9

m   64 × 8

Challenge

1   2   3   4   5   6   7   8   9

For each target number below, choose any three numbers from above once.

Arrange the numbers like this   ☐ ☐ × ☐
to make a product of:

a   445

b   448

c   450

d   608

e   536

f   639

Multiply the answer mentally, then record all the calculations.

Fabulous fifty

Practice

To multiply by 49 I think: Multiply by 50 and adjust

1 Calculate the answers to these. Show your working.

a 8 × 49   b 6 × 49

c 17 × 49   d 13 × 49

e 15 × 49   f 23 × 49

g 35 × 49   h 54 × 49

i 48 × 49   j 67 × 49

Example
12 × 49 = (12 × 50) − 12
        = 600 − 12
        = 588

To multiply by 51 I think: Multiply by 50 and adjust

Example
12 × 51 = (12 × 50) + 12
        = 600 + 12
        = 612

2 Calculate the answers to these. Show your working.

a 9 × 51   b 14 × 51

c 18 × 51   d 25 × 51

e 27 × 51   f 36 × 51

g 39 × 51   h 43 × 51

i 52 × 51   j 68 × 51

Refresher

Multiply each of the numbers below by 50, then write the new number.

Remember

× 100 then halve

Example
18 × 50 = 900
18 × 100 = 1800
half of 1800 = 900

a 36	b 14	c 23	d 40
e 28	f 19	g 47	h 33
i 42	j 54	k 68	l 90
m 76	n 58	o 65	p 84
q 82	r 72	s 96	t 93

Challenge

Joshua, Shamima and Ricardo each made a mosaic table.
They purchased their tiles from the same shop.
Find out who spent the most money.

TILE PRICES

51p each
49p each
50p for 2

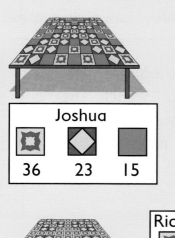

Shamima
44
20
25

Joshua
36 23 15

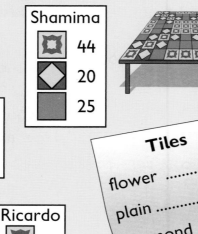

Ricardo
57
34

Tiles
flower ....
plain ....
diamond ....
TOTAL ....

1 Prepare an invoice for each person showing:
   a the total cost for each type of tile
   b the total cost for tiling the table
2 a Who spent the most money?
   b What was the difference between the cost of each of the tables?

17

Quick 17s

Practice

A quick way to multiply by 17

17 × 6 = (10 × 6) + (7 × 6)
= 60   + 42
= 102

1 Partition 17 into 10 and 7 to work out the answers.
   Show your working.

   a 17 × 9   **b** 17 × 15   **c** 17 × 6

   d 17 × 13   **e** 17 × 16   **f** 17 × 22

   g 17 × 25   **h** 17 × 31   **i** 17 × 28

   j 17 × 40   **k** 17 × 50   **l** 17 × 35

2 Read each story about 17. Choose an appropriate method
   of calculating your answer:

   ● mental

   ● mental with jottings (use the partition method)

a
The children at Oak Tree Primary School go swimming in groups of 17. There are 14 groups. How many children go swimming?

b
Over the summer term the 17 children from one Year 6 group went swimming 12 times. They pay 50p per lesson. What is the total amount paid by the group over the term?

c
The 17 new swimmers from Year 3 each buy a new swimming cap. Each cap costs 89p in the sale. What is the total amount spent on caps?

d
Each group of 17 children pay £25 each per term for their swimming lesson. What is the total cost per group?

e
Next year the cost per term for each child is to increase to £34. How much will it cost per group?

f
The shop sells goggles for £2·45 each. The Year 6 group buy a pair each. How much do they spend altogether?

Refresher

1 Multiply each of the numbers below by 10 and write the answer.

a 7   b 13   c 19   d 44   e 48

f 16   g 25   h 36   i 52   j 27

2 Multiply each of the numbers below by 7 and write the answer.

a 8   b 14   c 12   d 35   e 43

f 46   g 28   h 29   i 58   j 39

Challenge

The 17s Game

A game for 2 players

- a stopwatch
- calculator

33   65   17   44   29

12

1020	493	442	1105
289	884	561	867
646	748	765	204

17

51

60

38

52   45   26

What to do

1 Each player copies the centre grid.

2 Start the stopwatch.

3 Multiply the number cards by 17 to find the matching answer. Write the number from the number card above the correct number on the grid.

4 The first person to finish is the winner (but first check your answers using a calculator).

Villa division

Practice

Italy – Villa costs (per apartment, per week)			
	2 or 3 people	**4, 5 or 6 people**	**7, 8 or 9 people**
18 Mar – 14 Apr	295	385	445
15 Apr – 28 Apr	320	410	470
29 Apr – 23 Jun	355	430	485
24 Jun – 21 July	375	455	515
22 July – 18 Aug	630	750	865
19 Aug – 01 Sept	450	515	630
02 Sept – 29 Sept	390	450	505
30 Sep – 27 Oct	305	395	450

The travel agency has villas in Italy for rent. The cost of the villa depends on how many people will be staying and the date on which they travel. The agency has had many enquiries. Help them work out how much it will cost each person in the group.

Approximate your answer first. Record your answer using the standard method of division.

Enquiry No: 1
Date of travel: 20 April
No of people: 6
Villa cost:
Cost per person:

Enquiry No: 2
Date of travel: 27 July
No of people: 9
Villa cost:
Cost per person:

Enquiry No: 3
Date of travel: 12 August
No of people: 6
Villa cost:
Cost per person:

Enquiry No: 4
Date of travel: 20 May
No of people: 3
Villa cost:
Cost per person:

Enquiry No: 5
Date of travel: 31 August
No of people: 6
Villa cost:
Cost per person:

Enquiry No: 6
Date of travel: 12 October
No of people: 5
Villa cost:
Cost per person:

Enquiry No: 7
Date of travel: 15 August
No of people: 8
Villa cost:
Cost per person:

Enquiry No: 8
Date of travel: 3 July
No of people: 7
Villa cost:
Cost per person:

Enquiry No: 9
Date of travel: 27 June
No of people: 6
Villa cost:
Cost per person:

Refresher

Write a division fact for each number coming out of the machine and give the answer.

a
| 81 |
| 45 |
| 63 |
| 27 |
| 72 |

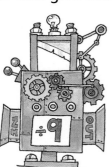

b
| 36 |
| 24 |
| 16 |
| 40 |
| 32 |

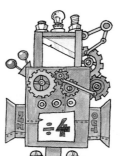

c
| 14 |
| 63 |
| 49 |
| 21 |
| 56 |

d
| 30 |
| 42 |
| 18 |
| 36 |
| 54 |

e
| 24 |
| 21 |
| 9 |
| 15 |
| 27 |

f
| 16 |
| 32 |
| 72 |
| 24 |
| 48 |

Challenge

DIY division calculations

- four 0–9 dice
- paper and pencil

Example

```
divisor    6 ) 743
               600     (100 × 6)
               143
               120     (20 × 6)
                23
                18     (3 × 6)
                 5
```

Answer = 123 5/6

What to do

Work with a partner

1 Take turns to throw the four dice. Choose one die as the divisor and put to one side.

2 Using the remaining 3 dice, both players make the largest 3-digit number possible.

3 Divide the 3-digit number by the divisor. Show your working and write any remainders as a mixed number.

4 Check your answer with your partner's work.

Division approximation

Practice

Approximate the answer first. Choose a standard method
of recording to work out the answer to each calculation.
Record any remainder as a mixed number.

Example

$376 \div 7 \approx 350 \div 7 = 50$

```
7 ) 376
    350      (50 × 7)
    ————
     26
     21      (3 × 7)
    ————
      5
```

Answer $= 53\frac{5}{7}$

Example

$376 \div 7 \approx 350 \div 7 = 50$

```
      53 5/7
7 ) 376
    35
    ———
    26
    21
    ———
     5
```

a $226 \div 3$

b $378 \div 4$

c $654 \div 9$

d $450 \div 6$

e $389 \div 8$

f $588 \div 8$

g $685 \div 7$

h $462 \div 5$

i $392 \div 6$

j $686 \div 8$

k $748 \div 9$

l $536 \div 7$

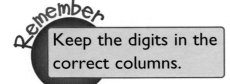

Remember

Keep the digits in the
correct columns.

Refresher

Work out the answers to these calculations.

a 48 ÷ 8
d 34 ÷ 5
g 240 ÷ 6
j 320 ÷ 8
m 280 ÷ 4
p 240 ÷ 3

b 63 ÷ 9
e 52 ÷ 6
h 350 ÷ 5
k 400 ÷ 5
n 210 ÷ 7
q 270 ÷ 9

c 47 ÷ 7
f 38 ÷ 4
i 720 ÷ 9
l 600 ÷ 6
o 160 ÷ 4
r 480 ÷ 8

Challenge

Divisibility tests

A number is divisible by:
2 if the last digit is 0, 2, 4, 6 or 8
3 if the sum of its digit is divisible by 3
4 if the tens and units digits divide exactly by 4
5 if the last digit is 0 or 5
9 if the sum of its digits are divisible by 9
10 if the last digit is 0

1 Ten of the answers in the maths book are incorrect. Use the divisibility tests and your skills of approximation to find them.

2 Work out the correct answers using the standard method of recording.

6 February 2000

a 2725 ÷ 5 = 545
b 762 ÷ 9 = 84
c 536 ÷ 4 = 134

d 458 ÷ 3 = 151
e 664 ÷ 4 = 166
f 351 ÷ 4 = 89

g 891 ÷ 9 = 99
h 3650 ÷ 5 = 730
i 452 ÷ 3 = 164

j 2644 ÷ 2 = 1322
k 3610 ÷ 10 = 361
l 786 ÷ 9 = 78

m 373 ÷ 4 = 84
n 4728 ÷ 2 = 2364
o 229 ÷ 3 = 73

p 687 ÷ 9 = 176
q 1630 ÷ 5 = 326
r 658 ÷ 9 = 72

s 844 ÷ 4 = 211
t 742 ÷ 3 = 147

Decimal division

Practice

The information labels below tell you what height a plant had grown to after a certain time period. Work out how much each plant grew on average in one week.

Approximate your answer first, then use the standard method of recording to calculate your answer. (Remember to line decimal points up under each other.)

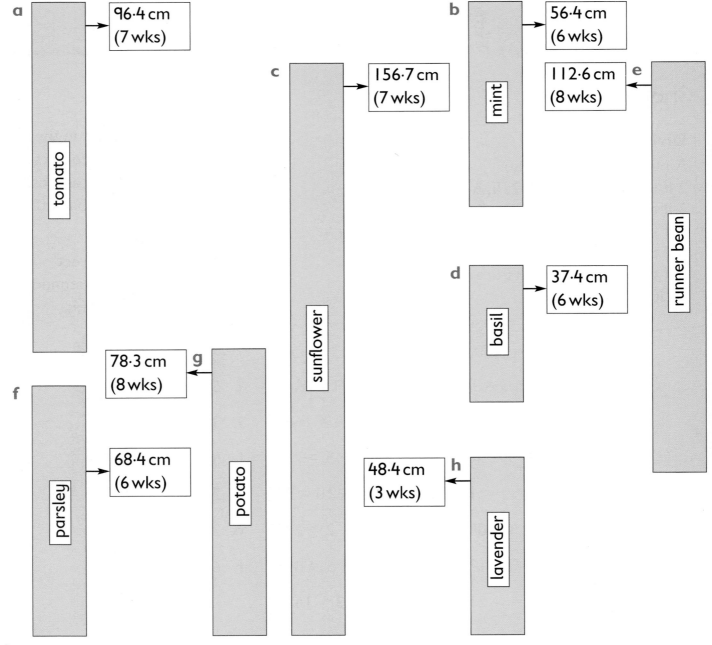

a tomato — 96·4 cm (7 wks)

b mint — 56·4 cm (6 wks)

c sunflower — 156·7 cm (7 wks)

e runner bean — 112·6 cm (8 wks)

d basil — 37·4 cm (6 wks)

g potato — 78·3 cm (8 wks)

f parsley — 68·4 cm (6 wks)

h lavender — 48·4 cm (3 wks)

Refresher

Approximate the answer to each calculation.

a 34·3 ÷ 3

d 28·3 ÷ 4

g 39·6 ÷ 4

j 28·7 ÷ 3

m 79·6 ÷ 9

p 46·2 ÷ 7

b 64·7 ÷ 6

e 37·5 ÷ 7

h 57·4 ÷ 8

k 83·6 ÷ 9

n 56·3 ÷ 10

q 39·7 ÷ 8

c 46·8 ÷ 5

f 16·8 ÷ 9

i 32·5 ÷ 5

l 47·2 ÷ 8

o 28·7 ÷ 2

r 66·2 ÷ 9

Challenge

Rearrange each set of 4 numbers to make a calculation in the form TU·t ÷ U to equal the answer shown on each label.

Example

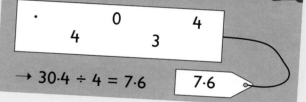

→ 30·4 ÷ 4 = 7·6   7·6

a
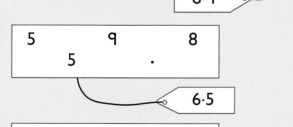
7   6   2
·   3
8·9

b
3   0   5
2   ·
6·4

c
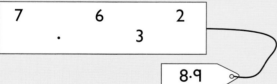
5   9   8
5   ·
6·5

d
·   4   0
3   8
3·8

e
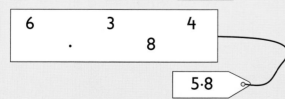
6   3   4
·   8
5·8

f
·   5   1
3   3
8·9

g
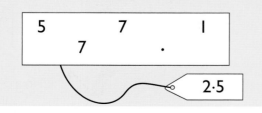
5   7   1
7   ·
2·5

h

·   4   3
2   9
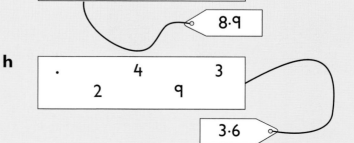
3·6

25

Holiday currencies

Practice

TOURIST RATES (June)			
Australia ($)	2·38	Malaysia (ringgits)	5·50
Austria (schillings)	20·97	Malta (lira)	0·62
Belgium (francs)	61·64	Mexico (nuevo peso)	13·67
Canada ($)	2·15	Netherlands (Guilders)	3·36
Cyprus (pounds)	0·87	New Zealand ($)	3·03
Denmark (kroner)	11·42	Norway (kroner)	12·62
Finland (markka)	9·12	Portugal (escudos)	305·77
France (francs)	9·96	Saudi Arabia (rials)	5·50
Germany (marks)	2·99	Singapore ($)	2·49
Greece (drachma)	514·87	South Africa (rand)	9·94
Hong Kong ($)	11·37	Spain (pesetas)	252·48
Ireland (punts)	1·20	Sweden (kroner)	12·68
India (rupees)	60·65	Switzerland (francs)	2·39
Israel (shekels)	5·75	Thailand (bahts)	54·36
Italy (lira)	2969	Turkey (lirasi)	900132
Japan (yen)	156·96	USA ($)	1·46

To convert pounds (£) into other currencies, multiply the number of pounds by the exchange rate.

1 Use the information in the "tourist rates" to find out how much of each of the currencies of the countries below you would receive when exchanging pounds. Copy and complete the table.

Country	Currency	Exchange rate	Round to nearest whole number	£5	£10	£25	£50	£100
Austria								
France								
Germany								
Greece								
Israel								
Spain								

To convert other currencies into pounds, divide the amount by the exchange rate.

2 While on holiday you buy some items. Use the exchange rates above to work out the cost of each item in English pounds. (Round each currency rate to the nearest whole number.)

a  Germany 763 DM

b Switzerland SF 35

c  Israel 26 sh

d Switzerland SF 7

e  France 83 FF

f  Hong Kong HK$ 220

g  Israel 166 sh

h  Hong Kong HK$ 132

Refresher

The Richards family are planning a holiday to Australia in July. There are two adults and three children aged 1 year, 8 years and 11 years. They need to purchase these things before they can travel.

Work out the total cost involved for the Richards family to fly to Australia.

Family travel insurance: £95

Air tickets

- Adults: £756
- Children under 12 years: £567
- Infants under 2 years: 25% off adult ticket price

Airport departure tax: £20 per person

Children under 2 years: half price

Challenge

Here are the "tourist rates" at a different time of the year.

1 Choose 15 countries to visit. Work out to see if the exchange rate has increased (↑) or decreased (↓) between April and June, and by how much.

2 Work out the difference between exchanging £10 in April and June. Write how much, and if it has increased (↑) or decreased (↓).

3 Decide when the better time to travel to each country would be based on this information.

TOURIST RATES (April)			
Australia ($)	2·57	Malaysia (ringgits)	5·72
Austria (schillings)	22·95	Malta (lira)	0·66
Belgium (francs)	67·46	Mexico (nuevo peso)	13·42
Canada ($)	2·25	Netherlands (Guilders)	3·67
Cyprus (pounds)	0·95	New Zealand ($)	3·09
Denmark (kroner)	12·49	Norway (kroner)	13·61
Finland (markka)	9·98	Portugal (escudos)	333·18
France (francs)	10·92	Saudi Arabia (rials)	5·72
Germany (marks)	3·28	Singapore ($)	2·55
Greece (drachma)	562·90	South Africa (rand)	10·31
Hong Kong ($)	11·80	Spain (pesetas)	276.95
Ireland (punts)	1·31	Sweden (kroner)	13·67
India (rupees)	61·55	Switzerland (francs)	2·63
Israel (shekels)	5·84	Thailand (bahts)	54·92
Italy (lira)	3249	Turkey (lirasi)	930029
Japan (yen)	165·21	USA ($)	1·52

4 Copy and complete the table to record your information. An example has been done for you.

Country	Exchange rate		↑ or ↓	Difference between exchanging £10 in April or June	Best time to travel
	April	June			
USA	1·52	1·46	↓ 0·06	·60 $US	April

Travel problems

Practice

Use the information on the flight adverts to answer the questions.

Return Fares from London to	
New York	£184
Florida	£247
Toronto	£265
Los Angeles	£267

New York City Break
3 nights from **£367**

1 a How much would it cost to travel one way to each destination?
   b What is the difference in cost between flights to New York and Los Angeles?
   c Work out how much the accommodation costs per night on the New York City Break.

Return Fares from London to	
Dubai	£255
Bangkok	£339
Hong Kong	£368
Singapore	£407

Thailand
8 nights from **£594**

2 a How much more does it cost to fly to Singapore than Dubai?
   b Calculate the one way fare to each of these destinations.
   c How much does the accommodation cost per night on the holiday in Thailand?

Return Fares from London to	
Jo'burg	£296
Cape Town	£352
Nairobi	£354
Durban	£514

Mauritius
5 nights from **£941**

3 a How much does the hotel package to Mauritius cost per night?
   b Half board (breakfast and dinner) costs 25% of the cost per night. How much does it cost? How much for the room only?

Return Fares from London to	
Sydney	£469
Auckland	£526
Perth	£560
Melbourne	£566

Australia
from **£538** Book by 30 June

4 a What is the difference between the normal return fare to Melbourne and the special fare?
   b Children under 12 pay 25% less than the adult fare. How much does it cost for a child to travel to each destination?
   c How much for a family of two adults and two children to fly to Perth?

Refresher

Look at the Return **fares** in the Practice section.

1. List the destinations shown in the adverts in the order of cost, beginning with the cheapest.

2. What is the difference in price between the cheapest flight and the most expensive flight?

3. Calculate the cost of three adults travelling to:
   a Toronto   b Hong Kong
   c Cape Town   d Auckland

4. Calculate the cost of six adults travelling to
   a New York   b Singapore
   c Nairobi   d Sydney

Challenge

Special: Round the World Fare £849.
Travel in the same direction. Take up to 1 year to complete.

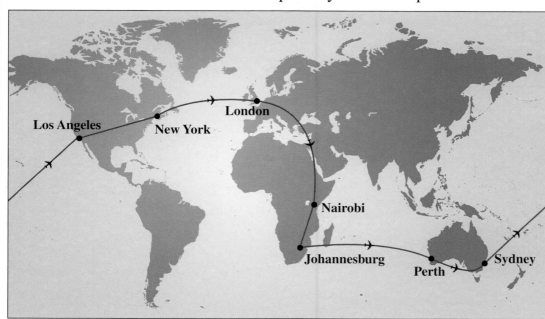

USA/CANADA RETURN FARES	
New York	£239
Boston	£239
Chicago	£239
Washington	£239
Los Angeles	£279
Las Vegas	£279
Miami	£269
Toronto	£265
Havana	£359
Mexico	£355

WORLDWIDE RETURN FARES	
Sydney	£465
Perth	£548
Auckland	£547
Bangkok	£327
Hong Kong	£348
Dubai	£362
Jo'Burg	£324
Cape Town	£357
Nairobi	£377

1. What is the difference in cost between travelling to each destination shown on the map on a separate trip starting each time at London, and taking a Round the World Fare?

2. The Travel Shop is offering a 50% discount on all return flights. Which option is cheaper? By how much?

Equivalent fractions

Practice

Order these fractions. First convert them to equivalent fractions then draw a number line and put the fractions on it.

a $\frac{5}{6}$ $\frac{2}{3}$ $\frac{1}{2}$ k $\frac{2}{6}$ $\frac{1}{4}$ $\frac{2}{3}$

b $\frac{3}{4}$ $\frac{2}{5}$ $\frac{6}{10}$ l $\frac{5}{8}$ $\frac{3}{4}$ $\frac{13}{16}$

c $\frac{3}{4}$ $\frac{2}{8}$ $\frac{3}{16}$ m $\frac{7}{9}$ $\frac{2}{3}$ $\frac{5}{6}$

d $\frac{2}{9}$ $\frac{1}{6}$ $\frac{1}{3}$ n $\frac{7}{10}$ $\frac{2}{5}$ $\frac{3}{4}$

e $\frac{5}{7}$ $\frac{1}{3}$ $\frac{2}{7}$ o $\frac{5}{10}$ $\frac{2}{5}$ $\frac{2}{6}$

f $\frac{2}{3}$ $\frac{1}{5}$ $\frac{3}{10}$ p $\frac{7}{9}$ $\frac{4}{6}$ $\frac{1}{2}$

g $\frac{9}{10}$ $\frac{4}{5}$ $\frac{3}{4}$ q $\frac{2}{3}$ $\frac{5}{9}$ $\frac{3}{4}$

h $\frac{3}{8}$ $\frac{1}{2}$ $\frac{2}{6}$ r $\frac{20}{24}$ $\frac{6}{8}$ $\frac{1}{3}$

i $\frac{1}{3}$ $\frac{5}{7}$ $\frac{2}{3}$ s $\frac{5}{18}$ $\frac{2}{6}$ $\frac{1}{9}$

j $\frac{7}{12}$ $\frac{3}{4}$ $\frac{4}{6}$ t $\frac{4}{7}$ $\frac{1}{2}$ $\frac{3}{4}$

Refresher

1 Order these fractions by first converting them to equivalent fractions. Then draw a number line and put the fractions on it.

   a $\frac{1}{2}$, $\frac{3}{5}$ convert to tenths

   b $\frac{1}{2}$, $\frac{3}{4}$ convert to eighths

   c $\frac{1}{2}$, $\frac{2}{3}$ convert to sixths

   d $\frac{2}{3}$, $\frac{4}{5}$ convert to fifteenths

   e $\frac{3}{6}$, $\frac{3}{4}$ convert to twelfths

   f $\frac{1}{4}$, $\frac{4}{5}$ convert to twentieths

2 Find the number that both denominators can divide into. Convert them to equivalent fractions. Then draw a number line and put the fractions on it.

   a $\frac{2}{3}$, $\frac{1}{4}$

   b $\frac{3}{4}$, $\frac{7}{10}$

   c $\frac{1}{2}$, $\frac{1}{3}$

   d $\frac{1}{4}$, $\frac{2}{5}$

   e $\frac{2}{3}$, $\frac{2}{5}$

   f $\frac{4}{6}$, $\frac{5}{9}$

   g $\frac{5}{8}$, $\frac{2}{3}$

Challenge

1 Copy this wall and complete it by adding together the two fractions below each brick. You will need to convert the fractions to the same denominator before you can add them.

2 Now copy and complete this fraction wall in the same way.

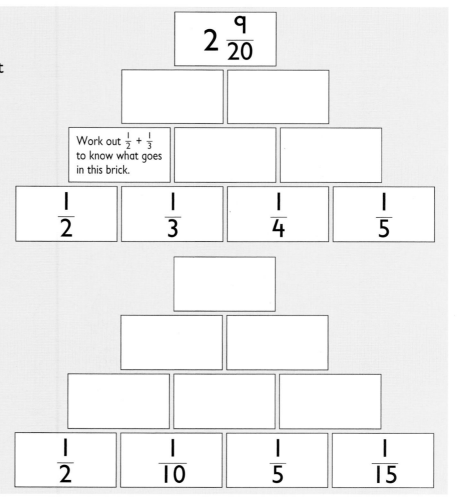

$2\frac{9}{20}$

Work out $\frac{1}{2} + \frac{1}{3}$ to know what goes in this brick.

$\frac{1}{2}$ $\frac{1}{3}$ $\frac{1}{4}$ $\frac{1}{5}$

$\frac{1}{2}$ $\frac{1}{10}$ $\frac{1}{5}$ $\frac{1}{15}$

Find the fraction

Practice

Find the fractions of these numbers and quantities.
You may want to use a calculator for some calculations.
Record your working out.

a $\frac{3}{10}$ of $\boxed{80}$, $\boxed{£50}$, $\boxed{120}$

b $\frac{46}{100}$ of $\boxed{3000}$, $\boxed{2600}$, $\boxed{£1500}$

c $\frac{5}{6}$ of $\boxed{600}$, $\boxed{120\,km}$, $\boxed{9\,m}$

d $\frac{3}{4}$ of $\boxed{51}$, $\boxed{900}$, $\boxed{266}$

e $\frac{2}{8}$ of $\boxed{448}$, $\boxed{112}$, $\boxed{3200\,m}$

f $\frac{2}{5}$ of $\boxed{400}$, $\boxed{£85}$, $\boxed{550}$

g $\frac{8}{10}$ of $\boxed{410}$, $\boxed{12\,m}$, $\boxed{1100}$

h $\frac{6}{100}$ of $\boxed{60\,m}$, $\boxed{4000}$, $\boxed{£5}$

i $\frac{2}{6}$ of $\boxed{31}$, $\boxed{3840}$, $\boxed{£96}$

j $\frac{5}{8}$ of $\boxed{£850}$, $\boxed{1608}$, $\boxed{592}$

Refresher

Find the fractions of these numbers and quantities.
You may want to use a calculator for some calculations.
Record your working out.

a $\frac{1}{4}$ of 440

b $\frac{1}{2}$ of 360

c $\frac{1}{3}$ of 312

d $\frac{1}{5}$ of 120

e $\frac{1}{4}$ of 96, $\frac{3}{4}$ of 96

f $\frac{1}{5}$ of 250, $\frac{3}{5}$ of 250

g $\frac{1}{6}$ of 60, $\frac{5}{6}$ of 60

h $\frac{1}{10}$ of 160, $\frac{4}{10}$ of 160

i $\frac{1}{100}$ of 400, $\frac{7}{100}$ of 400

j $\frac{1}{8}$ of 48, $\frac{6}{8}$ of 48

k $\frac{1}{4}$ of 8000, $\frac{3}{4}$ of 8000

l $\frac{1}{3}$ of 618, $\frac{2}{3}$ of 618

Challenge

Work out the fractions of the following measurements:

a $\frac{3}{10}$ of 2 m in centimetres?

b $\frac{23}{100}$ of 4 kg in grams?

c $\frac{7}{1000}$ of 1 m in millimetres?

d $\frac{7}{10}$ of 5 m in centimetres?

e $\frac{55}{100}$ of 7 l in millilitres?

Decimal decisions

Practice

1 Copy this table and fill in the tenths and whole numbers that the number in the middle is between. Circle the tenth and whole number it is closest to.

whole number	tenths	number	tenths	whole number
4	(4·6)	4·63	4·7	(5)
		7·92		
		3·49		
		0·51		
		8·75		
		9·16		
		22·06		
		45·99		
		31·39		
		17·28		
		34·72		
		58·51		

2 Order these decimals from smallest to largest.

a   5·23, 5·2, 5·36, 5·6, 5·32, 5·61

b   7·68, 7·66, 7·8, 7·86, 7·866, 7·066

c   2·001, 2·021, 2·21, 2·211, 2·202, 2·2

d   9·75, 9·57, 9·5, 9·771, 9·571, 9·7

e   21·4, 12·46, 21·406, 12·64, 12·4, 21·401

f   47·5, 47·05, 47·005, 47·15, 47·475, 47·015

g   84·1, 84·41, 84·441, 84·114, 84·4, 84·14

h   66·96, 66·99, 66·996, 66·9, 66·696, 66·6

i   0·412, 0·4, 0·21, 0·42, 0·224, 0·2

j   15·02, 15·26, 15·026, 15·6, 15·226, 15·262

Refresher

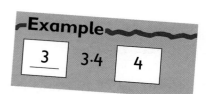
1 What whole numbers are these decimals between?
Underline the number the decimal is closest to.

a | ? | 4·8 | ? | b | ? | 5·6 | ? |

c | ? | 2·3 | ? | d | ? | 1·7 | ? |

e | ? | 9·2 | ? | f | ? | 4·56 | ? |

g | ? | 9·7 | ? | h | ? | 3·98 | ? |

i | ? | 7·49 | ? | j | ? | 6·52 | ? |

2 Order these decimals from smallest to largest.
   a 8·3, 8·6, 8·1, 8·7, 8·9, 8·2   b 2·26, 2·45, 2·78, 2·12, 2·95, 2·06
   c 5·62, 5·26, 5·66, 5·22, 5·06, 5·02   d 7·94, 7·96, 7·49, 7·07, 7·69, 7·99
   e 3·06, 3·03, 3·63, 3·36, 3·13, 3·31   f 9·5, 9·56, 9·6, 9·15, 9·67, 9·7
   g 2·6, 2·59, 2·8, 2·14, 2·87, 2·9   h 4·74, 4·47, 4·7, 4·4, 4·77, 4·89
   i 6·73, 6·51, 6·4, 6·82, 6·1, 6·9   j 12·81, 12·8, 12·63, 12·5, 12·77, 12·48

Challenge

I am thinking of a number…

1 If I count on 12 tenths I get to 4·8. What number am I thinking of?
2 If I count on 25 hundredths I get to 7·62. What number am I thinking of?
3 If I count on 30 hundredths I get to 10·21. What number am I thinking of?
4 If I count on 13 thousandths I get to 5·004. What number am I thinking of?
5 If I count on 24 thousandths I get to 13·473. What number am I thinking of?

What's the equivalent?

Practice

1 Copy and complete the following tables. Use a calculator to work them out if you need to. Record the calculation you use.
Write decimals to 2 decimal places.

a

fraction	equivalent decimal	calculation
$\frac{3}{4}$		
$\frac{2}{5}$		
$\frac{1}{3}$		
$\frac{1}{8}$		
$\frac{4}{8}$		
$\frac{4}{10}$		
$\frac{2}{3}$		
$\frac{4}{5}$		
$\frac{7}{8}$		

b

fraction	equivalent %	calculation
$\frac{3}{4}$		
$\frac{2}{5}$		
$\frac{1}{3}$		
$\frac{1}{8}$		
$\frac{4}{8}$		
$\frac{4}{10}$		
$\frac{2}{3}$		
$\frac{4}{5}$		
$\frac{7}{8}$		

2 Explain the link between fractions, decimals and percentages.

Refresher

1 Find the decimal equivalent to the following fractions.

   a $\dfrac{1}{2}$ b $\dfrac{1}{4}$ c $\dfrac{1}{5}$

   d $\dfrac{1}{8}$ e $\dfrac{1}{10}$ f $\dfrac{1}{100}$

> Remember you divide 1 by the denominator to find the decimal equivalent.

2 Now find the percentage equivalent.

> Remember you divide 100 by the denominator.

3 Find the decimal equivalent to the following fractions.

   a $\dfrac{5}{10}$ b $\dfrac{2}{5}$ c $\dfrac{36}{100}$ d $\dfrac{3}{4}$ e $\dfrac{8}{10}$

> Remember when the numerator is greater than 1 you divide 1 by the denominator then multiply the answer by the numerator.

4 Now find the percentage equivalent.

> Remember, divide 100 by the denominator then multiply the answer by the numerator.

Challenge

Find the decimal and percentage equivalents to the following fractions. You will need to round some of the decimals to two places. Use a calculator to help you.

   a $\dfrac{1}{9}$ b $\dfrac{1}{11}$ c $\dfrac{1}{12}$ d $\dfrac{1}{7}$ e $\dfrac{1}{15}$

Percentage wheels

Practice

Work out the percentages of the number in the centre of the wheel.
Record your method.

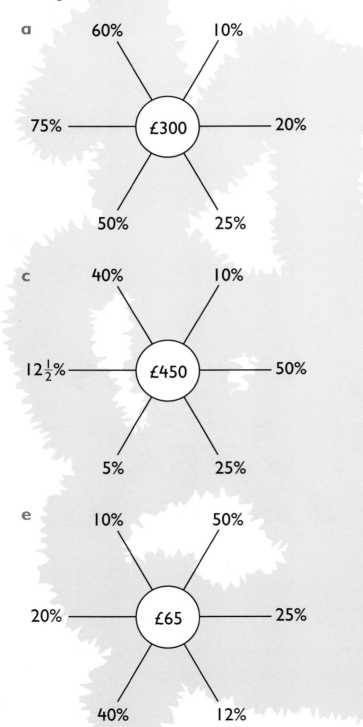

a

60%   10%

75% — £300 — 20%

50%   25%

c

40%   10%

$12\frac{1}{2}$% — £450 — 50%

5%   25%

e

10%   50%

20% — £65 — 25%

40%   12%

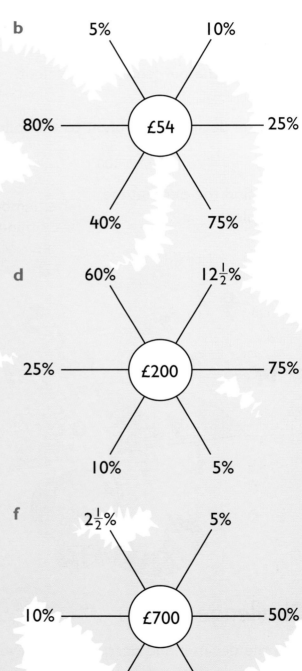

b

5%   10%

80% — £54 — 25%

40%   75%

d

60% $12\frac{1}{2}$%

25% — £200 — 75%

10%   5%

f

$2\frac{1}{2}$%   5%

10% — £700 — 50%

$12\frac{1}{2}$%   25%

Refresher

Find the percentages of these amounts. Use the answer to the first percentage to help you work out the second. Record your calculations.

a 50% of £800, 25% of £800

b 50% of £24, 25% of £24

c 50% of £620, 25% of £620

d 50% of £46, 25% of £46

e 10% of £70, 20% of £70

f 10% of £140, 20% of £140

g 10% of £300, 20% of £300

h 10% of £20, 40% of £20

i 10% of £480, 40% of £480

j 10% of £12, 40% of £12

Challenge

VAT is a tax that is added on to most things we buy.
At the moment VAT is always $17\frac{1}{2}$% of the price.
Work out a way to find $17\frac{1}{2}$% of these prices:

a £40

b £75

c £15

d £86

e £32

Circle patterns

Practice

You need:

● I cm square dot paper
● compasses
● pencil and eraser
● colouring materials

1 **a** Find the middle of your sheet of I cm
square dot paper. Set your compasses
to a radius of 5 cm and draw a circle.
Mark the centre O.

b Draw two circles, each with a centre
4 cm from O and with a radius of 3 cm.

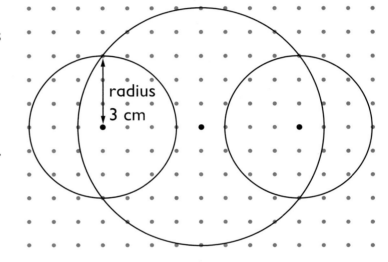

c Draw two more circles, moving the
centres I cm nearer to O and with a
radius of 4 cm.

d Draw another pair of circles, moving
the centres I cm nearer to O and
with a radius of 5 cm.

e Colour part of your design.

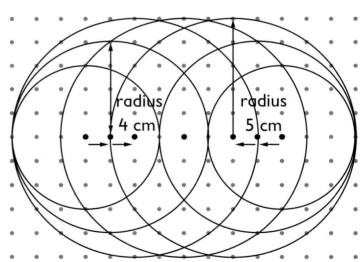

2 Design a similar pattern of your own.

Refresher

1   Construct a basic "hex" pattern.

   a Set your compasses to a radius of 4 cm and draw a circle.

   b Mark off the radius around the circumference.

   c Use a mark on the circumference as the centre of your circle. Draw an arc to cut the circumference twice.

   d Repeat 5 more times, using each point on the circumference. Erase the unwanted lines.

2   These designs are based on the "hex" pattern.

   Choose one to construct and colour.

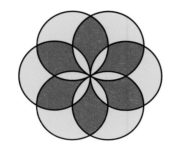

Challenge

1   Find a way to construct this basic pattern. PQRS is a square with sides of 6 cm. P, Q, R and S are the centres of circles with radius of 4 cm.

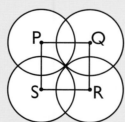
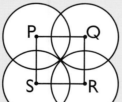

You need:
- compasses
- protractor or set square
- pencil and eraser
- ruler
- colouring materials

2   These designs are constructed from the basic pattern.

   Work out how each design has been made. Choose two to construct and colour.

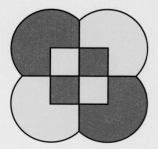

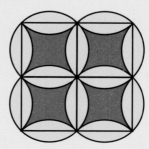

Looking at 3D shapes

Practice

1 Work with a partner. Each person copies the net of a half-tetrahedron on to 1 cm triangular dot paper.

2 Carefully cut out the net.

3 For each net:
   ● Score all dotted lines before folding.
   ● Fold up before gluing to visualise the solid.
   ● Glue the tabs in turn.

4 Find a way to place together the two half-tetradedra to form a tetrahedron. Glue both pieces together.

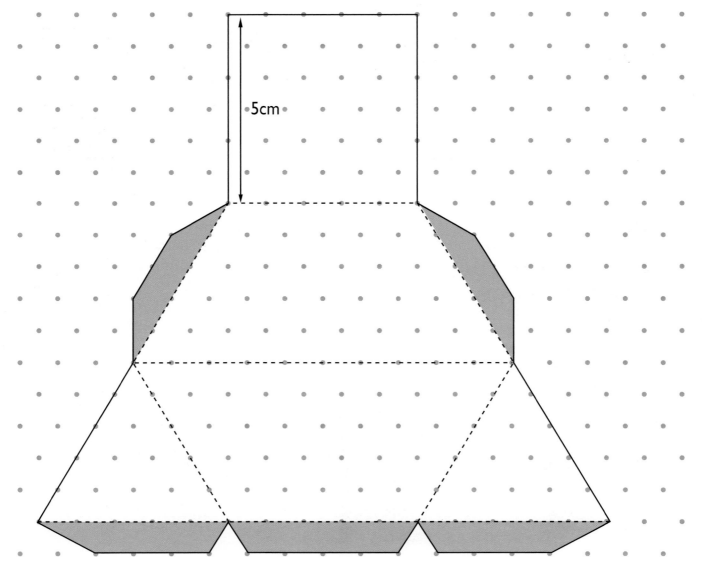

5cm

Refresher

cube

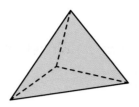
tetrahedron

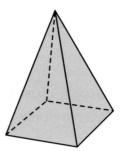
square-based pyramid

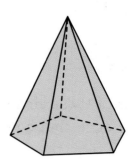
pentagonal pyramid

octahedron

dodecahedron

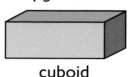
cuboid

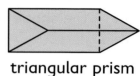
triangular prism

1 Work with a partner. For each question, write into which region, 1, 2 or 3, you would sort these solids:

a cube, tetrahedron, octahedron, pentagonal pyramid

no parallel edges		all faces congruent
1	2	3

b dodecahedron, triangular prism, square-based pyramid, cuboid

same number of edges at every vertex		at least one triangular face
1	2	3

Challenge

1 Work with a partner. Each person draws and cuts out the net of a square-based pyramid.

2 Find a way to glue the pieces together to make a "snap dragon" octahedron. Add the teeth and the eyes.

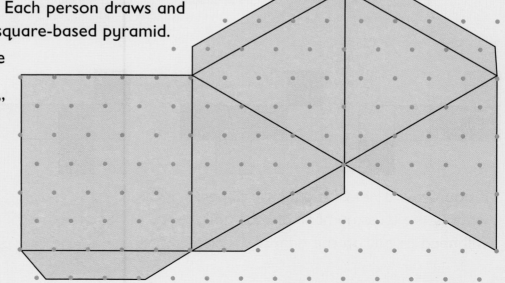

Check the net

Practice

You need:
● 6 interlocking square tiles

1 Some of these shapes are nets of a closed cube. Make each shape with your interlocking square tiles, then fold it up.

2 Copy and complete this table.
Enter ✓ if the shape is a net of a cube.
Enter ✗ if the shape is not.

shape	✓	✗
a	✓	
b		
c		

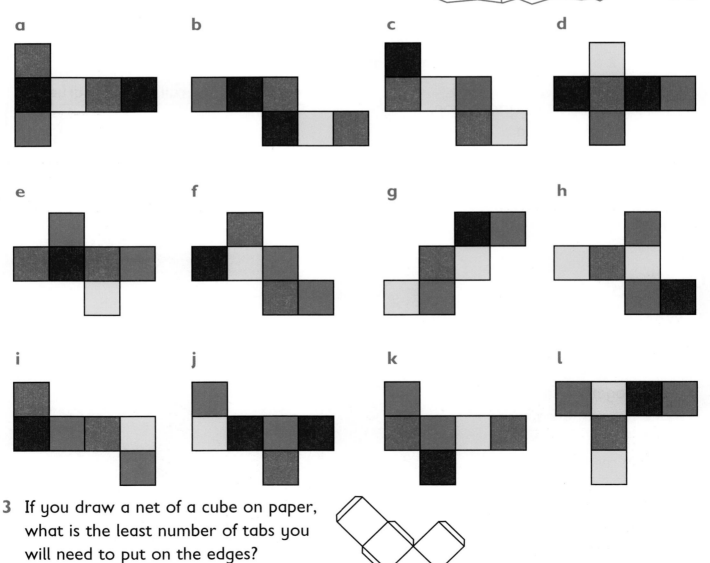

a   b   c   d

e   f   g   h

i   j   k   l

3 If you draw a net of a cube on paper, what is the least number of tabs you will need to put on the edges?

Refresher

You need:
● a die

These shapes are nets for five dice.

a   Copy each net on to 1 cm squared paper.
b   Fill in the missing dots so that opposite faces add up to 7.

a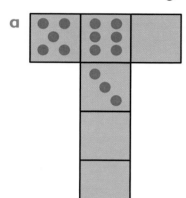

b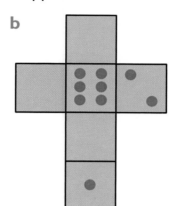

c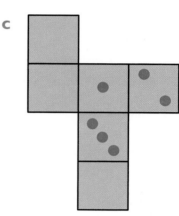

d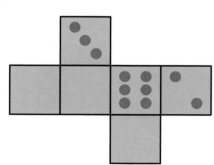

e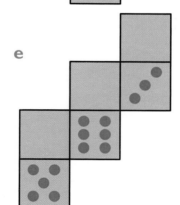

f

Challenge

a Make a 3 × 3 × 3 cube with 1 cm cubes.
   Now imagine all the outside faces painted blue.
b Find how many of the 1 cm cubes have:
   ● 0 blue faces
   ● 1 blue face
   ● 2 blue faces
   ● 3 blue faces
   ● 4 blue faces.
Do the same with a 4 × 4 × 4 cube and a 5 × 5 × 5 cube.

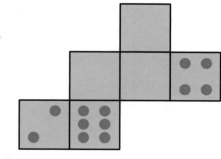

Terrific tangrams

Practice

1 Copy the square and tangram shapes on page 47 and label them A–G.

2 Using tangram pieces C, E and F, make:

   a a rectangle   **b** a parallelogram   **c** a trapezium

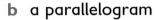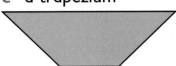

3 Make another trapezium using pieces D and G.

4 Use pieces C, D, E, F and G to make:

   a a square   **b** a hexagon

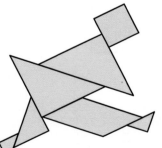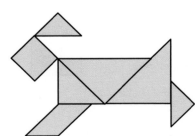

5 Using all 7 pieces, make:

   a a running man   **b** a house   **c** a dog   **d** a swan

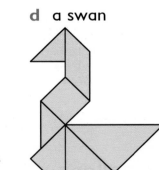

6 Here are some harder shapes to try. You may need two sets of the seven pieces.

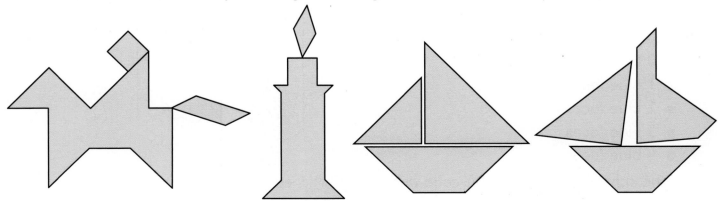

   a a man on a horse   **b** a candle   **c** two boats

Refresher

Copy the square and tangram shapes and label them A–G.

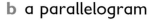

1 Make triangle A with shapes:

   a C, E and D.

   b C, E and F.

   c C, E and G.

2 a Make a square with 2 triangles.

   b Use the same 2 triangles to make a parallelogram.

3 Use all 7 tangram pieces to make:

   a a rectangle

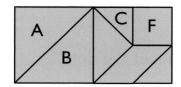

                                      b a parallelogram

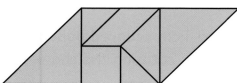

Challenge

All 7 tangram pieces will make a square. You can also make a larger "square with holes", again using all 7 pieces.

1 Make these shapes with:

   a a missing
     parallelogram

   b a missing
     triangle

2 There are more than 60 different ways to make a square with two triangles missing.

   a Make these "missing triangles" squares.

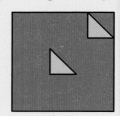
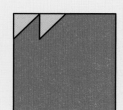

   b Try to find three more ways.

Rotate the shape

Practice

When you rotate a T-shape template through 90° about the point A, four times, you make this shape.

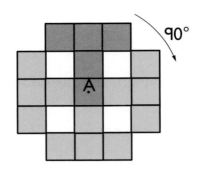

1 a Make templates of these shapes on 1 cm squared paper. Mark the point A.

b For each template, record on 1 cm squared paper, 4 rotations through 90° about the point A.

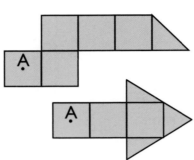

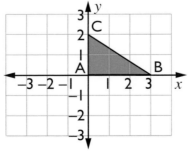

2 a Copy these shapes on to 1 cm squared paper.

b Complete each drawing by rotating the shape through 180° about the dot.

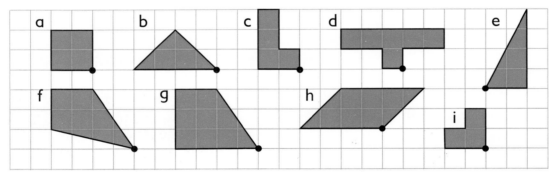

3 a Rotate the triangle ABC through 90° about the vertex A. Repeat the rotation 3 more times.

b Write the co-ordinates of B for each rotation.

4 Copy this shape on to squared paper. Write the co-ordinates of A, C, E and G.

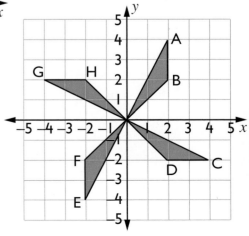

Refresher

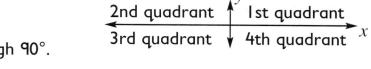

1 Make a pattern by rotating a shape through 90°.

a On a square of card, make cuts on 2 adjacent sides.

b Draw the x- and y-axes.

c Place the card in the 1st quadrant and draw round it.

d Rotate the card through 90°, into the 2nd quadrant, and draw round it.

e Repeat rotations of 90° into the 3rd and 4th quadrants.

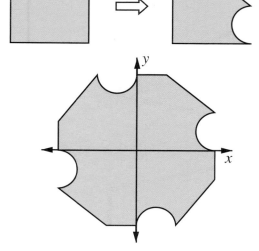

Challenge

1 Using 1 cm square dot paper, rotate the kite KLMN into the 4 quadrants.

2 Enter the co-ordinates of the vertices of each kite in a table.

vertex	quadrant			
	1st	2nd	3rd	4th
K	(1, 6)			
L	(3, 2)	(−2, 3)		
M		(−2, 5)		
N				

3 Write about any patterns you notice.

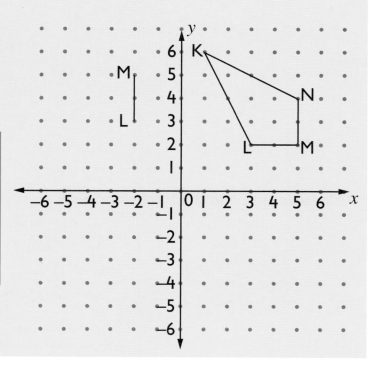

Measuring angles

Practice

1 The lines show the turns made by two skiers.
  Measure the angles along each ski trail to the nearest degree.

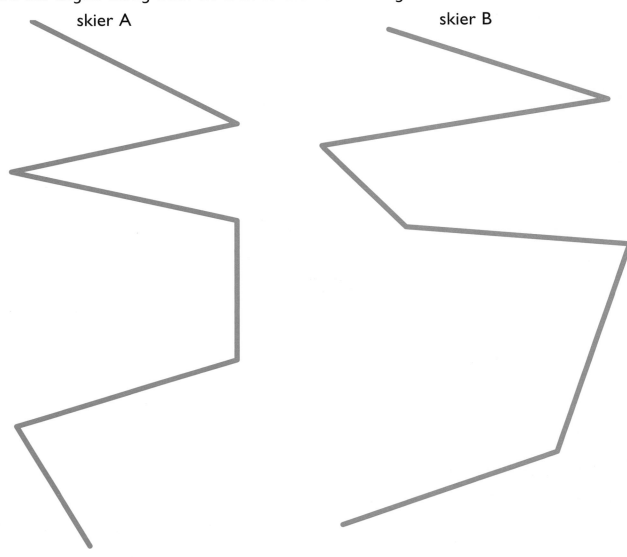

skier A

skier B

2 Measure and add the angles for each triangle.

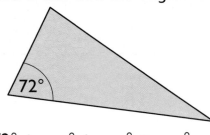

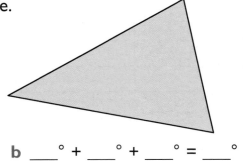

a 72° + ____° + ____° = ____°

b ____° + ____° + ____° = ____°

50

Refresher

These crisscross lines are fresh ski tracks in the snow.
Measure and record to the nearest degree the size
of each marked angle.

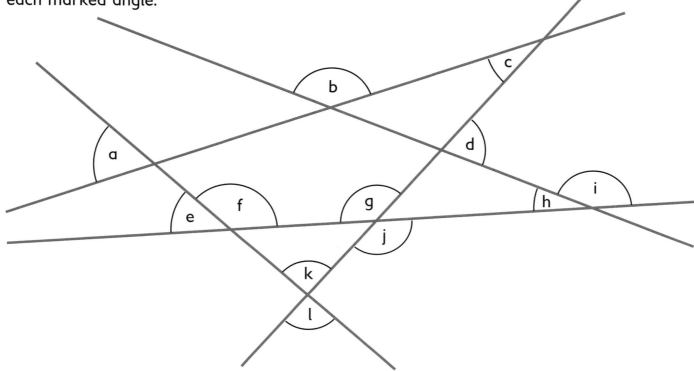

Challenge

Chalet roof puzzle

1 a Draw a large triangle for the
      roof of the chalet.
   b Mark the midpoints of the
      sides and join them up.
   c Measure all the angles in each
      of the 4 small triangles.
   d Write down what you notice.

2 What happens if you draw a
   different triangle? Will it still
   work? Investigate.

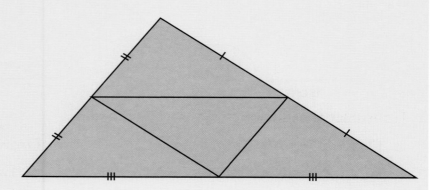

Drawing angles

Practice

1 Copy this table, then write the angles in the correct column:

acute	right	obtuse	straight	reflex
57°				

a 75°   b 157°   c 205°   d 340°   e 134°

f 180°   g 36°   h 90°   i 190°   j 275°

2 Draw and label angles of these sizes:

a 65°   b 137°   c 108°

d 42°   e 149°   f 161°

3 Make accurate drawings
of these angles.

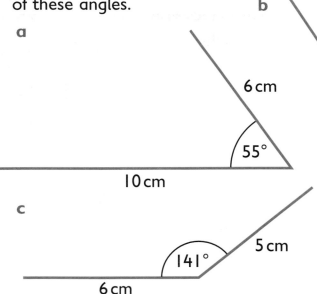

a

b   8 cm   6 cm   55°   10 cm

123°   10 cm

c   141°   5 cm   6 cm

d   10 cm   18°   8 cm

4 Construct these triangles.

a Draw a line AB 10 cm long.

● At A draw an angle of 40°.
● At B draw an angle of 65°.
● Extend the lines at A and B to
  meet at C.
● Measure the size of the angle at C.

b Draw a line PQ 8 cm long.

● Draw an angle of 57° at P and Q.
● Extend the lines at P and Q to
  meet at R.
● Measure the angle R.

Refresher

1 Work out the size of these angles on a compass rose.
Check with your protractor.

a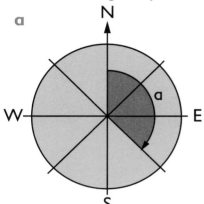

b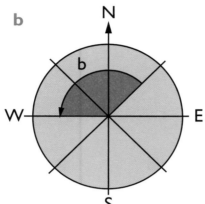

c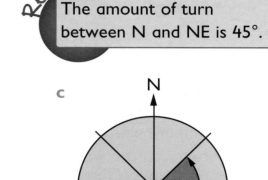

2 Write the direction in which you will face after turning through these reflex angles:

a Face west. Turn clockwise through 270°.
b Face north. Turn clockwise through 225°.
c Face east. Turn clockwise through 315°.
d Face SW. Turn anticlockwise through 270°.
e Face NE. Turn anticlockwise through 315°.

Example

Face south.

Turn clockwise through 270°.

You now face east.

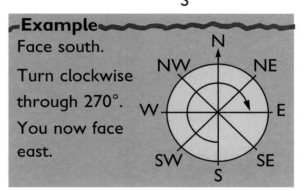

Challenge

1 Use the edge of your protractor to construct 5 semicircles from 0° to 180°.

Join the points at 0° and 180° to complete each semicircle.

2 For each semicircle:

a Mark a point on the circumference.

b Join the point to each end of the diameter line.

c Measure the angle at the circumference.

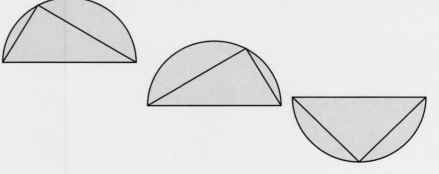

3 Make a general statement about the angle at the circumference of a semicircle.

Calculating angles

Practice

1 a PQR is a straight line. Measure and
   record the size of angles S and T.
   b One angle is 35°. What is the sum
   of angles S and T?
   c Compare with your measurements.
   How accurate were you?

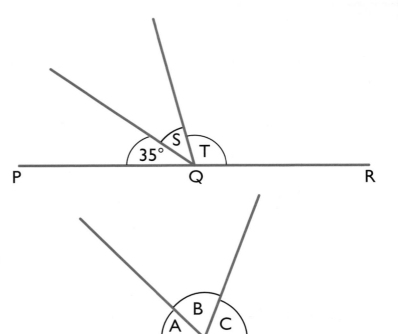

2 a Measure and record the size of
   angles A, B and C.
   b If DEF is a straight line, what should
   be the total of angles A + B + C?

3 First measure, then check by working out, the marked angles on these sails.

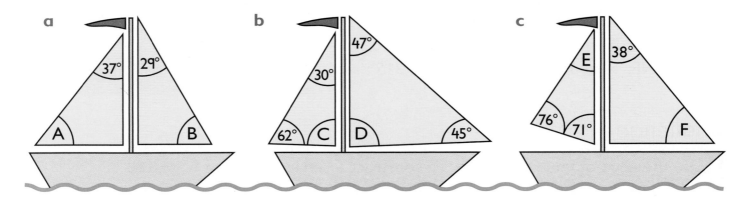

a

b

c

4 Name and calculate the sizes of the shaded angles.

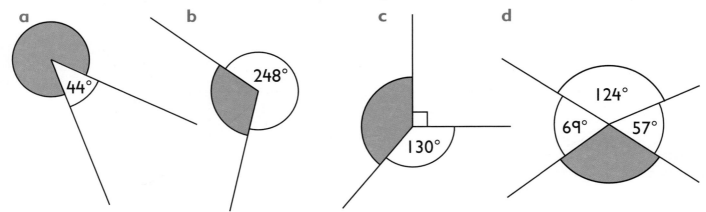

a

b

c

d

Refresher

1 These lines show the route of a bee from flower to flower.
Use your protractor to measure the size of the marked angles.

2 This trail – and some helpful clues – was left by a garden snail.

a Calculate the size of each missing angle.

b Now check your answers with your protractor.

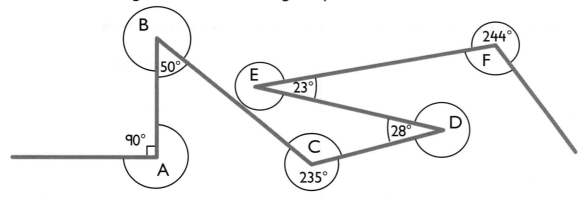

Challenge

1 Construct a regular pentagon which has sides of 6 cm and angles of 108°.

a

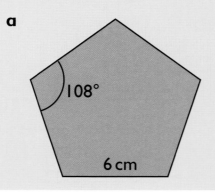

2 Construct a regular hexagon which has sides of 5·5 cm and angles of 120°.

b

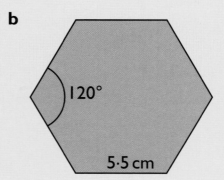

Find the area

Practice

You can work out the area of a shape in 3 different ways.

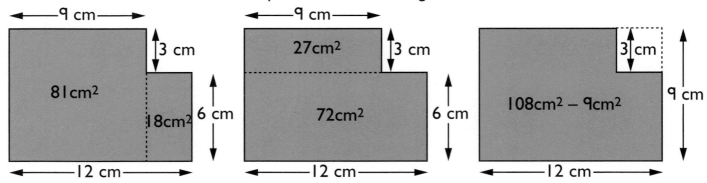

1 Calculate the area of each of these shapes.

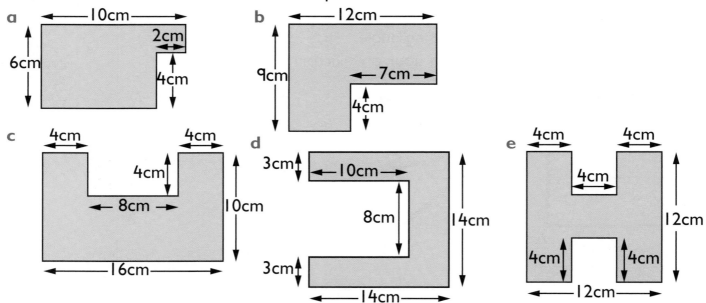

2 Work out the shaded area of each of these shapes.

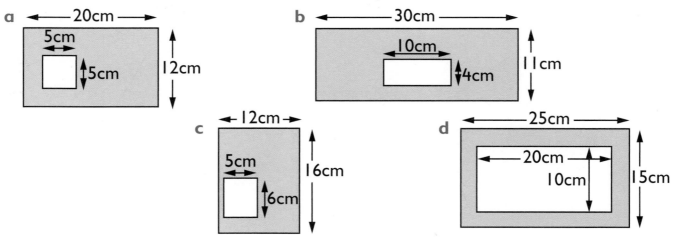

Refresher

Find the area of each of the shaded shapes in cm².

a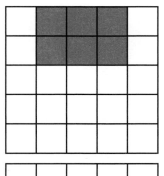
b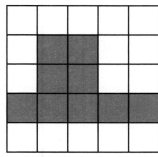
c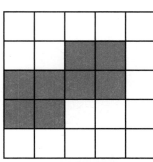

d
e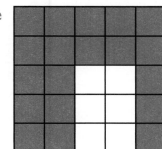
f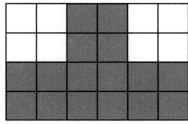

Challenge

1 Use centicubes to make these cubes.

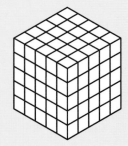

cube 1   cube 2   cube 3   cube 4

2 Copy and complete this table.

	cube 1	cube 2	cube 3	cube 4
surface area of one face	4 cm²			
surface area of cube	24 cm²			

3 Look for a pattern in the table and use it to work out the surface area of cubes with sides of 10 cm, 15 cm, 50 cm.

4 Find a way to calculate the surface area of each parcel.

 3cm 3cm 5cm

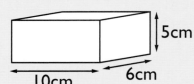 5cm 10cm 6cm

57

Calculating areas

Practice

1 Work out the area of the red shapes.

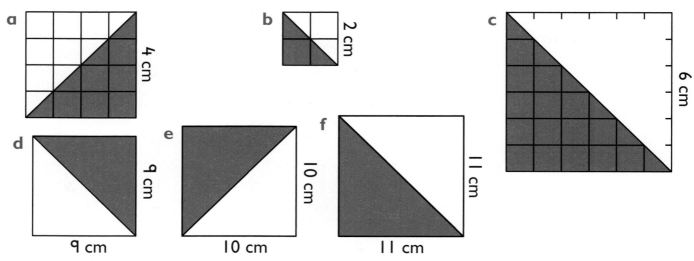

a   4 cm

b   2 cm

c   6 cm

d   9 cm · 9 cm

e   10 cm

f   11 cm · 10 cm

2 Change each right-angled triangle into a square and find its area.

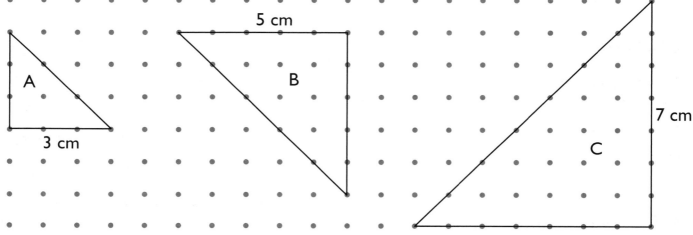

A   3 cm

5 cm   B

C   7 cm

3 Find the area of the tangram square.

4 Find the area of these tangram pieces:
   a triangle A + triangle B
   b triangle A
   c triangle C
   d triangle G
   e square F

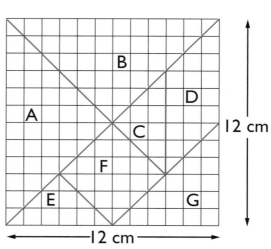

12 cm

12 cm

Refresher

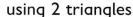

using 2 triangles	using 3 triangles	using 4 triangles

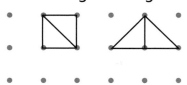 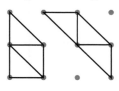 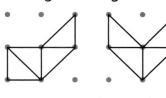

area = $1\,cm^2$ area = $1\frac{1}{2}\,cm^2$ area = $2\,cm^2$

1 You need 4 identical right-angled triangles. Use them to make these shapes, then record your answers on 1 cm square dot paper.
  a Take 2 triangles. Find 1 more shape with an area of $1\,cm^2$.
  b Take 3 triangles. Find 2 more shapes which have areas of $1\frac{1}{2}\,cm^2$.
  c Take 4 triangles. Find 8 more shapes with areas of $2\,cm^2$.

2 a Draw 3 different shapes which are made by joining 5 right-angled triangles.
  b Work out the area of each shape.

Challenge

These shapes all have 8 pins on their perimeter. Some have no pins inside, some have one pin and some, two or more.

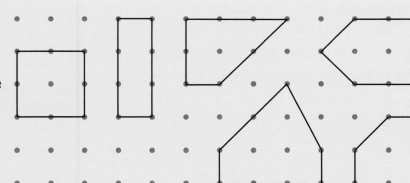

1 On 1 cm square dot paper, make different shapes which have 8 pins on their perimeter. Work systematically beginning with 0 pins inside, 1 pin inside, 2 pins inside, etc. Copy and complete the table.

Number of pins inside	0	1	2	3	4	5
Area in cm^2	3					

2 Use the table to predict the area of shapes with 6 pins inside and 10 pins inside. Make a general statement about the relationship between the number of pins inside the shape and its area.

Areas of right-angled triangles

Practice

1 Calculate the areas of these right-angled triangles.

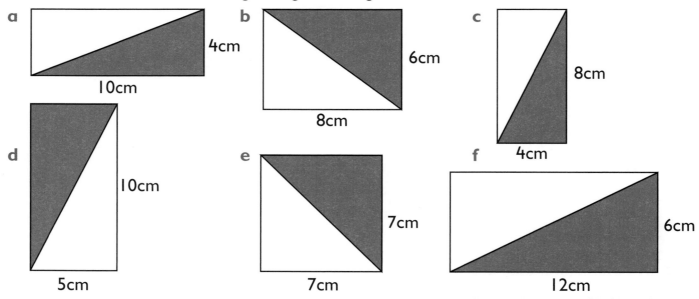

a 10cm, 4cm
b 8cm, 6cm
c 8cm, 4cm
d 10cm, 5cm
e 7cm, 7cm
f 12cm, 6cm

2 a Copy each triangle below on to 1 cm squared paper and cut it out.
  b Transform the triangle into a rectangle and paste it into your exercise book.
  c Find the area of the transformed shape.

Example

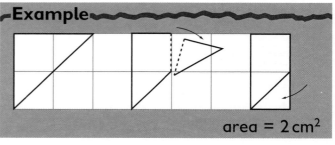

area = 2 cm²

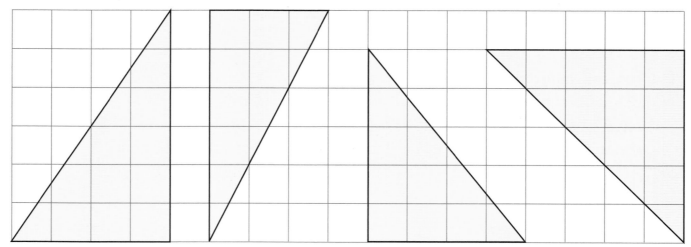

3 On 1 cm squared paper, draw two different right-angled triangles which have an area of 10 cm².

Example

Example

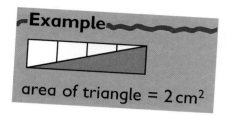

area of triangle = 2 cm²

Refresher

1 Work out the area of each triangle.

a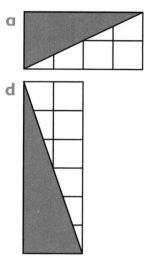

b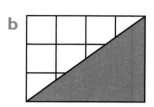

c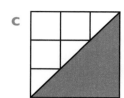

f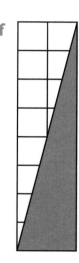

d

e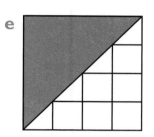

2 Write the letter of the triangle which has the same area as:

a triangle b

b triangle e

Challenge

Copy each pentagon on to 1 cm squared paper.
Now find a way to work out the area of
each pentagon.

Hint: Decide where to
draw lines to divide the
pentagon into rectangles
and triangles.

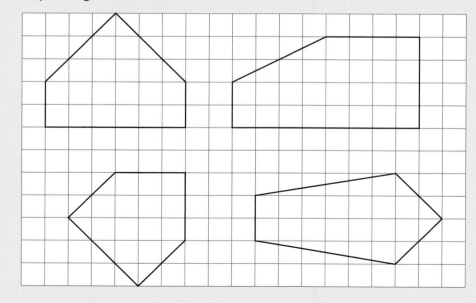

Whale weights

Practice

1 Round the weight of these whales to the nearest tenth of a kilogram, then to the nearest kilogram. Copy and complete the table.

weight	rounded to nearest $\frac{1}{10}$ kg	rounded to nearest kg
83·635 kg	83·6 kg	84·0 kg
a 46·270 kg		
b 67·475 kg		
c 59·520 kg		
d 70·090 kg		
e 112·875 kg		
f 111·040 kg		
g 94·760 kg		

2 Copy and complete this table which shows the average weight of adult whales.

	whale	tonnes	kilograms
a	blue whale	150 t	150 000 kg
b	sei whale	20 t	
c	humpback whale	25 t	
d	killer whale (male)		9000 kg
e	killer whale (female)		6400 kg
f	narwhal	1·5 t	
g	minke whale	8 t	
h	sperm whale		57 000 kg
i	pygmy sperm whale		400 kg
j	dwarf sperm whale		210 kg

3 Find how many times heavier the blue whale is than:

a the humpback whale   b the narwhal   c the pygmy sperm whale

Refresher

1 Change these weights to decimal notation.

a $\frac{3}{10}$ kg, $\frac{3}{100}$ kg, $\frac{3}{1000}$ kg

b $\frac{6}{10}$ kg, $\frac{6}{100}$ kg, $\frac{6}{1000}$ kg

2 Change these weights to fractional notation.

a 0·9 kg, 0·09 kg, 0·009 kg

b 0·7 kg, 0·07 kg, 0·007 kg

3 Copy and complete.

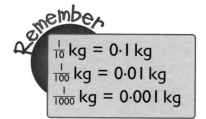

Remember

$\frac{1}{10}$ kg = 0·1 kg

$\frac{1}{100}$ kg = 0·01 kg

$\frac{1}{1000}$ kg = 0·001 kg

plastic pen caps	weight
1000	1 kg or 1·0 kg
100	$\frac{1}{10}$ kg or ___ kg
—	___ kg or 0·01 kg
1	$\frac{1}{1000}$ or ___ kg

Challenge

1 Calculate, in kilograms:

a The weight of krill a blue whale will eat in one day.

b The difference between the average and heaviest recorded weights of a blue whale.

2 A slice of pizza for a human weighs 0·2 kg. How many times larger would the pizza slice have to be for the appetite of an average blue whale?

3 What is the approximate weight of a one-month old baby blue whale?

Facts about blue whales

• The largest living creatures on Earth.

• The average weight is about 150 tonnes.

• The heaviest-ever caught weighed about 190 tonnes.

• The daily consumption of krill, small sea creatures similar to shrimp, is about 4 tonnes.

• Birth weight is about 3000 kg.

• A baby blue whale puts on about 100 kg in weight each day.

Backpack weights

Practice

Six children are going on a school trip.
The weight of each backpack is given below.

Delroy	Meera	Tom	Jenny	Sam	Amy
5·248 kg	5·813 kg	6·478 kg	4·685 kg	8·157 kg	7·589 kg

1 Write the number of grams represented by the 8 digit in the
   backpacks of Meera, Tom, Jenny and Sam.

2 Round each weight to the nearest tenth of a kilogram,
   then to the nearest kilogram. Copy and complete the table.

Backpack	Rounded to nearest $\frac{1}{10}$ kg	Rounded to nearest kg
Delroy	5·2 kg	5 kg
Meera		
Tom		
Jenny		
Sam		
Amy		

3 Find the difference in weight, in grams, between these backpacks:

   a Delroy's and Tom's   b Meera's and Sam's
   c Jenny's and Amy's   d the lightest and the heaviest

Refresher

1 Look at the weight of each backpack on the opposite page.
Write each weight as:

a kilograms and grams　　　　　b grams only

Example
Delroy's pack:

5·284 kg　= 5 kg 248 g
　　　　　= 5248 g

2 Delroy used these weights to weigh his backpack. In the same way,
work out which weights were used to weigh the other 5 backpacks.

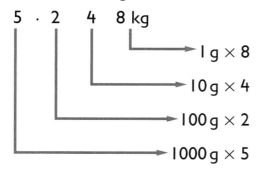

5 · 2　4　8 kg

→ 1 g × 8
→ 10 g × 4
→ 100 g × 2
→ 1000 g × 5

Challenge

1 Find which three backpacks will weigh the same as the combined
weight of Sam's and Amy's pack.

2 Jenny and Amy are twins. If they decide to rearrange their bags
so that each will carry the same weight, how many grams will
Amy give to Jenny to carry?

Pounds and ounces

Practice

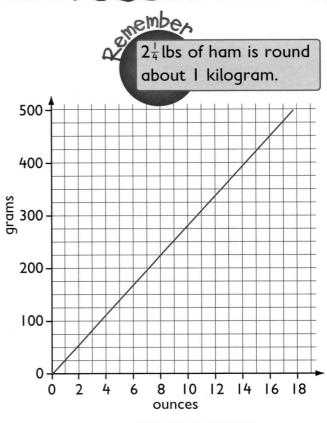

Remember

$2\frac{1}{4}$ lbs of ham is round about 1 kilogram.

1 Copy and complete.

1 lb ≈ 454 g

$\frac{1}{2}$ lb ≈ ☐

$\frac{1}{4}$ lb ≈ ☐

$\frac{3}{4}$ lb ≈ ☐

2 Use the conversion table to work out these answers.

Round the figures to the nearest ounce or gram.

a 7 oz ≈ ☐ g

b ☐ oz ≈ 30 g

c 14 oz ≈ ☐ g

d 2 lb ≈ ☐ g

e ☐ oz ≈ 250 g

f ☐ oz ≈ 380 g

3 Copy and complete the table.

Item	Metric	Imperial
cornflakes	500 g	_____
marmalade	340 g	_____
butter	_____	7 oz
tin of tuna	90 g	_____
tea	_____	$\frac{1}{4}$ lb
bread	_____	$1\frac{3}{4}$ lb

4 Kate wants to knit a sweater for her baby brother.
The old knitting pattern which she got from her gran needs five 1 oz balls of wool.
If knitting wool is sold in balls of 50 g,
how many balls of wool will she need to buy?

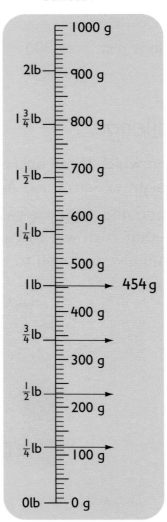

Refresher

1 Copy and complete these tables.

a 1 pound = 16 ounces

1 quarter pound = [ ] ounces

1 half pound = [ ]

3 quarters of a pound = [ ]

b 1 lb = 16 oz

$\frac{1}{4}$ lb = [ ] oz

$\frac{1}{2}$ lb = [ ]

$\frac{3}{4}$ lb = [ ]

2 Write **true** or **false** for each statement.

Use the conversion table on the opposite page to check each answer.

> **Example**
> 2 lb is less than 1000 g. True

a 1 lb is about 450 g

b $\frac{1}{2}$ lb is more than 200 g

c 4 oz rounds up to 100 g

d 12 oz rounds down to 300 g

e 8 oz > 200 g

f $\frac{1}{4}$ lb < 100 g

g 2 lb is just over 900 g

h 1000 g < 16 oz

Challenge

The imperial system of weights used this series of numbers:

1, 2, 4, 8, 16, 32 .... and so on.

> **Example**
> weight of apples = (1 + 4 + 8
> = 45 oz

Write the least number of weights you need to balance an object weighing:

a 11 oz

b 15 oz

c 23 oz

d 30 oz

e 43 oz

f 47 oz

g 55 oz

h 62 oz

i 70 oz

Weights workout

Practice

The table gives the weight of each daily and Sunday newspaper.

Newspaper	Weight
Daily Times	270 g
Herald	300 g
Morning Express	350 g
Daily News	250 g
Post on Sunday	400 g
Sunday News	500 g

1 Calculate the weight in kilograms of newspapers delivered to each house in one week.

	Address	Daily (Mon–Sat)	Sunday	Total in kg
	4 Thorn Road	Morning Express	Sunday News	2·1kg + 0·5kg = 2·6kg
a	7 Briar Avenue	Herald	Post on Sunday	
b	35 Ash Grove	Daily Times	Sunday News	
c	60 Oak Lane	Daily News, Herald	Sunday News	
d	48 Elm Crescent	Morning Express, Daily Times	Post on Sunday	
e	16 Willow Way	Herald, Daily News	Sunday News	

2 At the start of Pat's paper round, his bag weighs 7·35 kg. He has 5 copies of the Daily Times, 6 of the Herald, 7 of the Morning Express and the rest are the Daily News.

How many copies of the Daily News does he deliver?

3 Peter delivers 17 copies of Post on Sunday and 13 copies of Sunday News to 20 houses.

a How many customers take two Sunday newspapers?

b How heavy is his bag at the start of his Sunday paper round?

68

Refresher

1 The table shows the number of copies of each paper ordered by two newsagents.

Using a calculator, work out the weight, in kilograms, of paper delivered to each newsagent's shop.

Copy and complete the table.

Newspaper	Weight	Newsagent 1		Newsagent 2	
		Copies	Weight	Copies	Weight
Daily Times	270 g	20	5·4 kg	30	___ kg
Herald	300 g	50	___ kg	75	___ kg
Morning Express	350 g	30	___ kg	50	___ kg
Daily News	250 g	60	___ kg	40	___ kg
		Total weight	___ kg	Total weight	___ kg

2 Find the difference in the total weight of newspapers ordered by the two shops.

Challenge

1 Kenny, Liam and Mike each have a newspaper round.
The combined weight of their three bags of papers is 21 kg.
Kenny's bag is 600 g lighter than Liam's.
Liam's bag and Mike's bag are exactly the same weight.

What is the weight of each boy's bag?

2 Make up a similar problem for a friend to solve.

Multiplication line graphs

Practice

You need:
● graph paper
● a ruler

1 Copy and complete this 6 times multiplication table.

$0 \times 6 = 0$
$1 \times 6 =$
$2 \times 6 =$
$3 \times 6 = 18$
$4 \times 6 =$
$5 \times 6 =$
$6 \times 6 =$
$7 \times 6 =$
$8 \times 6 =$
$9 \times 6 =$
$10 \times 6 =$

2 Copy and complete the line graph for your table.

Mark each point using a cross. The point for 3×6 has been done for you.

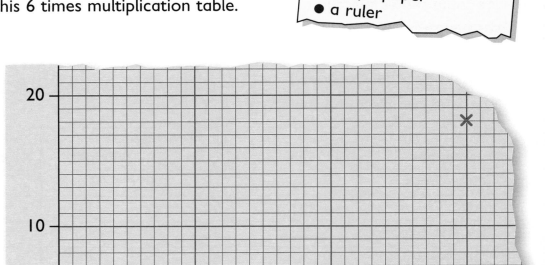

3 Use your graph to answer these calculations.

a $1\frac{1}{2} \times 6 =$ b $8\frac{1}{2} \times 6 =$ c $4\frac{1}{2} \times 6 =$

d $3 \cdot 5 \times 6 =$ e $9 \cdot 5 \times 6 =$ f $7 \cdot 5 \times 6 =$

g $54 \div 6 =$ h $33 \div 6 =$ i $15 \div 6 =$

4 Ribbon costs 6p a metre. How much do these children spend altogether?

a Marva buys 3·5 m, John buys 7 m.

b Charlie buys 2·5 m, Alec buys 9·5 m, Antionette buys 5 m.

c Jason buys 6·5 m, Uwana buys 1·5 m, Karen buys 5·5 m.

d Harold buys 12·5 m.

e Liam buys 14·5 m, Sharon buys 16 m.

You need:
● squared paper
● a ruler
● red and green pens

Refresher

1 Copy and complete this 4 times multiplication table.

$0 \times 4 = 0$
$1 \times 4 =$
$2 \times 4 =$
$3 \times 4 = 12$
$4 \times 4 =$
$5 \times 4 =$
$6 \times 4 =$
$7 \times 4 =$
$8 \times 4 =$
$9 \times 4 =$
$10 \times 4 =$

2 Copy and complete the line graph for the 4 times table. Mark each point using a cross.

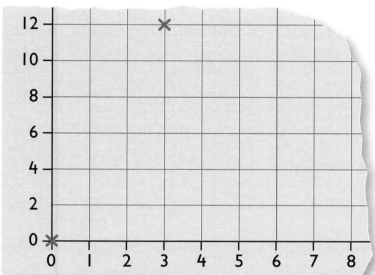

3 Use a red pen to circle the crosses for these calculations.

   a $3 \times 4 = 12$ b $9 \times 4 = 36$ c $7 \times 4 = 28$

4 Use a green pen to circle the crosses for these calculations.

   a $8 \div 4 = 2$ b $32 \div 4 = 8$ c $24 \div 4 = 6$

Challenge

You need:
● graph paper
● a ruler

1 Draw a line graph for the 7 times multiplication table.

2 Use your graph to answer these questions.

   a $1\frac{1}{2} \times 7$ b $8\frac{1}{2} \times 7$ c $4\frac{1}{2} \times 7$

   d 3.5×7 e 9.6×7 f 7.2×6

3 Estimate the answers to these.

   a $40 \div 7$ b $52 \div 7$ c $19 \div 7$

4 Cheese costs £7 per kg. Using the line graph, work out how much these people spend altogether.

   a Gavin buys 3·5 kg, Iris buys 2 kg.

   b Lana buys 2·8 kg, Francis buys 9·3 kg, Lesley buys 3 kg.

   c Kulbir buys 4·6 kg, Lin buys 1·2 kg, Jessi buys 5·7 kg.

Distance-time graphs

Practice

This graph shows a train journey for the **City Flyer** from Welbon to Ibury to Welbon.

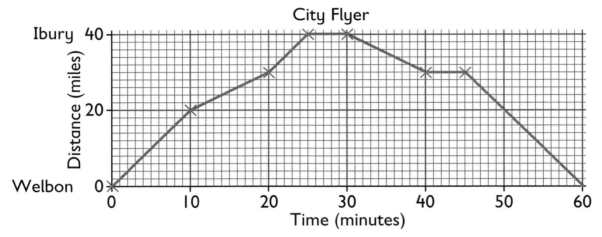

1 When was the City Flyer these distances from Welbon:

   a 30 miles going   b 36 miles going   c 20 miles returning

2 How far was the City Flyer from Welbon at these times:

   a 5 minutes   b 28 minutes   c 48 minutes

3 This table shows the distances and times for the **Express** from Welbon to Ibury.

   Copy and complete the distance-time graph.

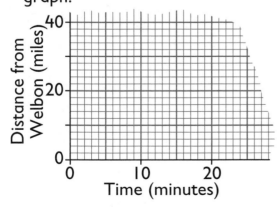

Express

Time (minutes)	Distance from Welbon (miles)
0	0
10	10
15	20
20	20
30	25
35	15
50	0

4 When was the Express these distances from Welbon:

   a 5 miles going   b 21 miles going

5 How far was the Express from Welbon at these times:

   a 25 minutes   b 12 minutes

You need:
- squared paper
- a ruler

Refresher

1 This table shows the distances and times for a motorcycle journey from Pilsea to Lissy and back to Pilsea. Copy and complete the distance-time graph.

Time (minutes)	Distance from Pilsea (km)
0	0
10	15
20	25
25	35
35	35
45	15
60	0

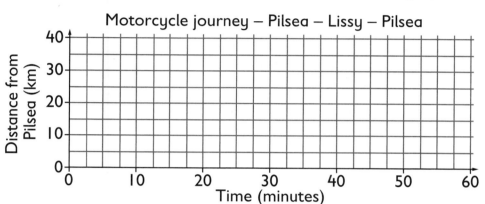

Motorcycle journey – Pilsea – Lissy – Pilsea

2 How far was the motorcycle from Pilsea at these times?

a 15 minutes　　b 30 minutes　　c 40 minutes　　d 55 minutes

Challenge

The diagram shows two spaceships travelling between two space stations.

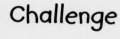

Alpha　　G2　　K2000　　Beta

Time (days)	Distance from Alpha (km)	
	G2	K2000
0	0	4500
1	500	4000
2	1000	4000
3	3000	3500
4	3000	2000
5	4000	1000
6	4000	1000
7	4500	0

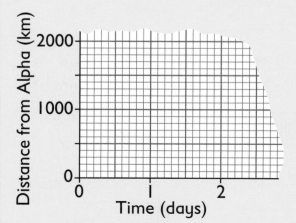

Draw a distance-time graph for each spaceship on the same axes.

Conversion graphs

Practice

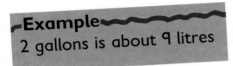

You need:
● graph paper
● a ruler

This graph converts between gallons and litres. Use it to estimate the answer to these questions.

Example
2 gallons is about 9 litres

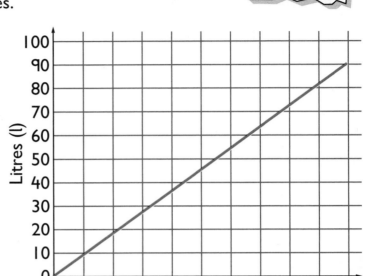

1 Convert these to litres.

    a 6 gallons   b 14 gallons

    c 5 gallons   d 17 gallons

2 Convert these to gallons.

    a 90 litres   b 30 litres

    c 70 litres   d 20 litres

3 Copy and complete this table of values.

Gallons	Litres (l)
0	0
2	9
4	18
6	
8	
10	

4 Use your table to draw a conversion graph on graph paper. Turn your graph paper sideways.

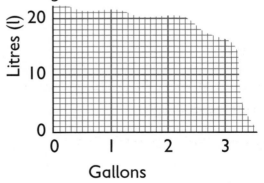

Use your graph to answer these questions.

5 How many litres does each drum contain?

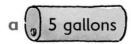 a 5 gallons   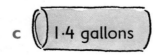 b 9 gallons   c 1·4 gallons   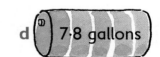 d 7·8 gallons

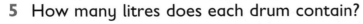
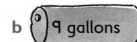

6 How many gallons does each drum contain?

 a 15 litres   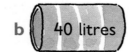 b 40 litres   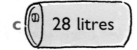 c 28 litres    d 34 litres

You need:
- squared paper
- a ruler

Remember

I kg is about 2 lb.

Refresher

1 Copy and complete this table.

kilograms (kg)	pounds (lb)
0	
1	
2	
3	
4	
5	
6	
7	
8	

2 Use your table to complete this graph.

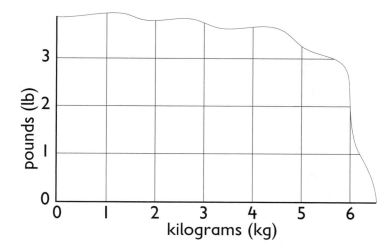

Use your graph to answer these questions.

3 Convert these weights to pounds.

a 2·5 kg   b 7·5 kg   c 1·5 kg   d 4·5 kg

4 Convert these weights to kilograms.

a 11 lb   b 1 lb   c 13 lb   d 7 lb

Challenge

You need:
- graph paper ● a ruler
- a calculator

1 1 kg is almost exactly 2·2 lb. Copy and complete the table.
   Use your calculator.

kilograms (kg)	pounds (lb)
0	
10	
20	
30	
40	
50	
60	
70	
80	

2 Use your table to draw a conversion graph.
   Use these scales for the axes: horizontal axis 2 cm
   to 10 kg; vertical axis 2 cm to 20 lb.
   Use your graph to answer these questions.

3 Convert these weights to pounds.

   a 25 kg   b 17 kg   c 62 kg   d 43 kg

4 Convert these weights to kilograms.

   a 120 lb   b 36 lb   c 94 lb   d 142 lb

75

Vertical addition

Practice

1 Write these calculations vertically and then work out the answer.

a 48 723 + 9614   b 83 715 + 28 624

c 72 417 + 3894   d 63 891 + 2584

e 75 129 + 58 421   f 3651 + 82 496

g 4637 + 81 284   h 36 527 + 23 945

i 48 326 + 47 391   j 59 823 + 14 965

k 7593 + 24 863   l 45 381 + 9578

m 158 496 + 35 821   n 758 236 + 48 362

o 163 954 + 478 531   p 963 158 + 239 647

q 85 136 + 743 085   r 7631 + 813 624

s 863 247 + 7230

2 Add these three numbers together using the vertical method.

a 48 632 + 593 + 1578   b 2678 + 3691 + 28 749

c 392 + 47 695 + 3825   d 48 + 9247 + 63 814

e 862 + 3954 + 58 432   f 15 823 + 3145 + 1587

g 49 + 48 762 + 69 854   h 85 713 + 5482 + 632

i 899 + 3621 + 58 472   j 30 452 + 6259 + 457

Refresher

1 Test yourself! Write the answers to these addition calculations as quickly as you can.

a 12 + 6   b 9 + 8   c 7 + 4   d 2 + 13

e 15 + 3   f 8 + 6   g 5 + 9   h 11 + 7

i 12 + 8   j 4 + 8   k 13 + 5   l 7 + 6

m 9 + 9   n 14 + 5   o 2 + 16   p 4 + 15

2 Write these calculations out vertically
and then work out the answer.

Example
```
  6847
+ 3059
------
  9906
   11
```

a 3642 + 5183   b 5627+ 2649   c 4085 + 5376

d 6243 + 5375   e 9481 + 352   f 8732 + 539

g 76 589 + 3072   h 36 781 + 2906 i 43 374 + 4917

j 52 476 + 9153   k 27 635 + 45 125   l 53 962 + 24 971

Challenge

Add these numbers using the vertical method.

a 45 + 3687 + 28 954 + 487 263   b 78 541 + 691 523 + 48 327 + 154

c 759 316 + 4829 + 86 + 763   d 9 + 6859 + 793 845 + 692 + 785 169

e 957 824 + 6953 + 482 + 8 + 83 174   f 785 + 693 184 + 7256 + 7 + 59

g 8079 + 91 532 + 73 + 480 635 + 631   h 385 + 18 965 + 8475 + 896 584 + 709

Vertical decimals

Practice

1 Copy the calculations out vertically and work out the answer.

a 15·487 + 32·721

b 39·47 + 83·29

c 146·86 + 48·69

d 4·954 + 15·752

e 725·63 + 47·15

f 483·92 + 74·6

g 4583·9 + 143·92

h 692·8 + 63·704

i 80·437 + 7·71

j 8·43 + 164·22

k 6921·5 + 751·78

l 7596·4 + 83·15

m 752·62 + 4852·32

n 9621·4 + 3678·88

o 63·781 + 932·7

p 9·663 + 87·63

2 Add these three numbers together in the same way.

a 38·48 + 51·957 + 3·54

b 7·548 + 36·45 + 7259·4

c 721·8 + 36·842 + 3·874

d 2631·7 + 6·485 + 1·36

e 423·84 + 3·801 + 60·771

f 183·425 + 84·04 + 8·777

g 71·823 + 614·4 + 8·003

h 823·14 + 85·744 + 5831·5

i 63·75 + 444·8 + 1005·7

j 76·14 + 7·88 + 8·152

k 9002·4 + 71·312 + 8·459

l 6·77 + 5·162 + 7824·3

m 1963·4 + 853·72 + 74·63

n 8·774 + 64·9 + 1532·23

o 20·44 + 81·753 + 6073·2

p 13·651 + 4·09 + 102·45

Refresher

1 Write the number that goes with each decimal to equal 1

  a 0·4   b 0·6   c 0·1   d 0·7   e 0·9

  f 0·2   g 0·5   h 0·3   i 0·8

2 Copy the calculations out vertically and work out the answer.

  a 5·87 + 36·84   b 96·61 + 19·55   c 73·47 + 26·61

  d 85·12 + 48·33   e 81·29 + 28·32   f 157·6 + 81·7

  g 395·7 + 42·1   h 347·6 + 83·7   i 48·7 + 211·3

  j 75·2 + 504·4   k 2·581 + 85·374   l 44·921 + 2·847

  m 41·951 + 84·267   n 2·305 + 43·617   o 92·364 + 5·311

Challenge

Using the digits 4, 5, 6, 7, 8 and 9 make these totals by adding two numbers together. In each calculation each digit may only be used once.

  a 9·596   b 66·36   c 485·4

  d 73·29   e 13·26   f 104·34

Example
To make 77·25
I need to add
7·85
69·4
77·25

Vertical subtraction

Practice

Write these calculations vertically and then work out the answer.

a 35 245 − 4189

b 76 314 − 8271

c 96 217 − 8477

d 70 831 − 5925

e 66 314 − 8207

f 75 641 − 9073

g 48 502 − 6723

h 55 817 − 8204

i 34 251 − 6314

j 75 123 − 942

k 85 633 − 708

l 968 423 − 48 621

m 604 238 − 76 214

n 306 087 − 24 321

o 719 625 − 8421

p 962 147 − 8467

q 15 219 − 5841

r 762 183 − 7610

s 64 283 − 5073

t 672 514 − 8447

u 88 452 − 9175

v 69 874 − 814

w 793 597 − 409

x 556 347 − 8200

y 148 264 − 38 499

z 268 745 − 919

Refresher

1 Test yourself! Write the answers to these subtraction calculations as quickly as you can.

a 18 − 6   b 15 − 7   c 13 − 8   d 9 − 4

e 11 − 5   f 17 − 9   g 16 − 7   h 15 − 11

i 19 − 15   j 18 − 12   k 20 − 7   l 14 − 9

2 Write these calculations vertically and then work out the answer.

a 9523 − 821   b 8172 − 3645   c 9720 − 1813   d 7389 − 5093

e 9148 − 523   f 5791 − 834   g 6872 − 491   h 57 219 − 3705

i 62 977 − 4838   j 74 684 − 3971   k 43 972 − 5318   l 39 783 − 7825

Challenge

How many different subtraction calculations can you write that will give you an answer of ...

Example

```
   8 5 1
  9̶6̶ ̶3̶8̶5̶
− 47 660
  48 725
```

48 725

I used the vertical method to help me find what to subtract from 96 385 to equal 48 725.

Be creative!

More vertical decimals

Practice

Write each calculation vertically and work out the answer.

a 62·48 − 14·8

b 157·8 − 84·57

c 2471·85 − 367·4

d 982·67 − 31·962

e 7821·8 − 391·87

f 507·68 − 89·791

g 4631·87 − 108·6

h 42·591 − 7·31

i 6074·9 − 294·16

j 75·91 − 8·63

k 143·84 − 51·726

l 18·421 − 9·47

m 7542·8 − 634·87

n 479·21 − 51·8

o 6372·8 − 483·69

p 4805·1 − 698·83

q 843·9 − 25·167

r 739·14 − 73·662

s 7114·5 − 43·81

t 507·43 − 77·327

u 1068·6 − 106·49

v 29 736·74 − 452·8

w 891·542 − 38·4

x 7810·6 − 521·66

y 652·94 − 48·61

z 6732·4 − 298·72

Refresher

1 Write the number that goes with each decimal to equal 10.

a 5·1 b 8·6 c 7·4 d 9·5

e 1·8 f 2·7 g 3·3 h 7·9

i 1·4 j 6·5 k 0·6 l 5·4

2 Write each calculation vertically
and work out the answer.

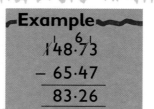

Example

$$\overset{\scriptstyle 1}{1}\overset{\scriptstyle 6}{4}8\overset{\scriptstyle 1}{\cdot}73$$
$$-\ 65\cdot47$$
$$\overline{83\cdot26}$$

Remember to
include the
decimal point
in the answer!

a 84·67 − 52·36 b 157·8 − 106·2 c 97·481 − 26·381

d 204·8 − 38·9 e 187·61 − 57·16 f 319·57 − 126·38

g 167·82 − 67·08 h 483·91 − 76·37 i 28·624 − 15·814

j 751·44 − 108·19 k 67·48 − 20·67 l 821·7 − 59·3

m 196·72 − 80·39 n 75·19 − 26·24 o 181·75 − 84·66

Challenge

Work out what needs to be subtracted from each number
to get to the next number. Record your answers as calculations.

a 426·75 ➤ 207·17 ➤ 159·72 ➤ 28·42

b 84·279 ➤ 51·437 ➤ 23·718 ➤ 9·104

c 1573·5 ➤ 954·8 ➤ 504·7 ➤ 331·6

Sums and differences

Practice

1 Add the two 2–digit numbers together, then use the
   answer to help work out the other calculations.

   a 62 + 37   b 58 + 49   c 86 + 35   d 94 + 22
      0.62 + 0.37   0.58 + 0.49   0.86 + 0.35   0.94 + 0.22
      6·2 + 3·7   5·8 + 4·9   8·6 + 3·5   9·4 + 2·2
      620 + 370   580 + 490   860 + 350   940 + 220
      6200 + 3700   5800 + 4900   8600 + 3500   9400 + 2200

2 For these calculations write out the other four calculations yourself.

   a 76 + 84   b 88 + 92   c 27 + 80   d 38 + 47

   e 59 + 28   f 63 + 43   g 31 + 95   h 57 + 92

3 Subtract the 2–digit numbers from each other, then use
   the answer to help work out the other calculations.

   a 83 – 57   b 92– 37   c 68 – 35   d 79 – 17
      0·83 – 0·57   0·92 – 0·37   0·68 – 0·35   0·79 – 0·17
      8·3 – 5·7   9·2 – 3·7   6·8 – 3·5   7·9 – 1·7
      830 – 570   920 – 370   680 – 350   790 – 170
      8300– 5700   9200 – 3700   6800 – 3500   7900 – 1700

4 For these calculations write out the other four calculations yourself.

   a 65 – 28   b 72 – 37   c 93– 45   d 89 – 31

   e 53 – 17   f 87 – 41   g 90 – 63   h 74 – 23

Refresher

1 Write the number that goes with each decimal to equal 0·1

a 0·04   b 0·06   c 0·01   d 0·07   e 0·09

f 0·02   g 0·05   h 0·03   i 0·08

2 Add and subtract these two-digit numbers mentally as quickly as you can.

a 48 + 37   b 41 + 28   c 37 + 68   d 25 + 79   e 64 + 81

f 97 − 51   g 84 − 67   h 76 − 34   i 54 − 31   j 57 − 29

3 Add and subtract the two 2-digit numbers then use the
answer to help work out the other calculations.

a 37 + 46	b 19 + 25	c 58 + 24	**Example**
370 + 460	190 + 250	580 + 240	48 + 31 = 79
3700+ 4600	1900 + 2500	5800 + 2400	480 + 310 = 790
			4800 + 3100 = 7900

d 68 + 17   e 71 − 52   f 85 − 38   g 92 − 45
680 + 170   710 − 520   850 − 380   920 − 450
6800 + 1700   7100 − 5200   8500 − 3800   9200 − 4500

Challenge

Explain how you can use the addition and subtraction of 2-digit
numbers to work out other calculations. Give examples to illustrate
your explanation. Do you think this is useful or not? Why?

Multiples of 100

Practice

1 Work out these addition calculations.

a 5100 + 2300

b 3300 + 4800

c 6500 + 3000

d 7200 + 1600

e 4300 + 1900

f 8400 + 6300

g 7800 + 2600

h 9300 + 2100

i 7700 + 4500

j 8300 + 4100

2 Work out these subtraction calculations.

a 7500 − 2100

b 8400 − 6300

c 9700 − 2700

d 7600 − 1900

e 3800 − 1300

f 7600 − 4300

g 9900 − 5100

h 7500 − 3800

i 9700 − 7100

3 What is the missing number in these calculations?

a 7300 − ? = 2200

b ? + 5400 = 7800

c 9800 − ? = 3500

d ? − 3700 = 5300

e ? + 5900 = 9800

f 8400 − ? = 1500

g 6300 + ? = 9600

h ? − 2600 = 8400

i 8700 − ? = 1200

j ? + 8400 = 12 400

4 Choose one addition and one subtraction calculation from each section and explain how you worked them out.

Refresher

Choose two numbers below and make an addition and subtraction calculation with them. Do this 15 times, using a different combination of numbers each time.

7500	6300	2400

3600

8100

9500

1100

9600

5500

8400

7300

6200

6200

4700

3900

2200

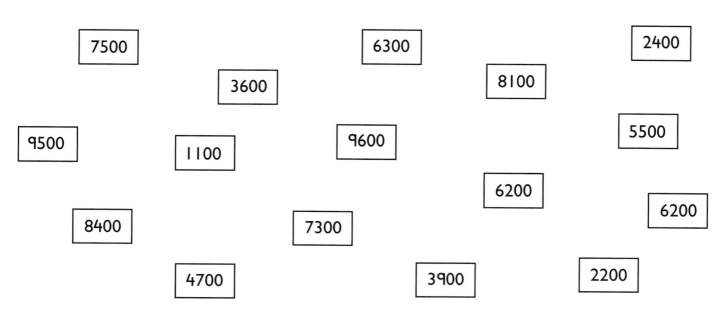

Challenge

Rolling 100s game

You need:
- two 0–9 dice
- paper and pencil each

What to do

1. Playing in pairs, take it in turns to roll the dice. You can read the two numbers either way. So if you roll a 3 and a 7 it can be 37 or 73.

2. Times your number by 100 to make a four-digit multiple of 100, for example, 3700 or 7300.

3. Write your number down on your piece of paper. Each time you roll a new number you add it on.

4. The winner is the first person to reach 50 000 exactly.

Decimals demonstration

Practice

1 Work out what needs to be added to these decimals to get to the next tenth.

Example
8·37 + 0·03 = 8·4

a 4·51	b 0·82	c 3·67	d 2·58
e 5·73	f 8·16	g 7·25	h 7·84
i 3·29	j 7·64	k 8·67	l 3·18

2 Work out what needs to be added to these decimals to get to the next whole number.

Example
8·37 + 0·63 = 9

a 4·82	b 6·71	c 3·67	d 0·91
e 2·54	f 7·38	g 5·23	h 6·15
i 9·48	j 4·02	k 6·84	l 3·11

3 Work out these decimal calculations. You might want to change the **tenths** to **hundredths**.

a 0·3 + 0·25	b 0·4 + 0·31	c 0·18 + 0·7	d 0·33 + 0·2
e 0·2 + 0·63	f 0·4 + 0·59	g 0·82 + 0·6	h 0·73 + 0·7
i 0·9 + 0·31	j 0·74 + 0·8	k 0·84 – 0·2	l 0·5 – 0·31
m 0·9 – 0·16	n 0·24 – 0·1	o 0·46 – 0·3	p 0·68 – 0·5
q 0·7 – 0·44	r 0·8 – 0·11	s 0·7 – 0·06	t 0·67 – 0·2

Refresher

1 Write the number that goes with these numbers to make 100.

   a 48   b 34   c 29   d 17

   e 35   f 44   g 92   h 52

   i 73   j 69   k 82   l 95

2 Work out what needs to be added to these numbers to equal
   the next tenth and the next whole number.

a 3.21   + ☐ = 3.3
            + ☐ = 4

b 4.52   + ☐ = 4.6
            + ☐ = 5

c 1.85   + ☐ = 1.9
            + ☐ = 2

d 2.34   + ☐ = 2.4
            + ☐ = 3

e 5.17   + ☐ = 5.2
            + ☐ = 6

f 3.19   + ☐ = 3.2
            + ☐ = 4

g 2.73   + ☐ = 2.8
            + ☐ = 3

h 5.46   + ☐ = 5.5
            + ☐ = 6

i 2.82   + ☐ = 2.9
            + ☐ = 3

3 Work out these decimal calculations.

   a 0.7 + 0.1   b 0.5 + 0.3   c 0.2 + 0.4   d 0.8 − 0.4

   e 0.9 − 0.6   f 0.5 − 0.1   g 0.78 + 0.11   h 0.41 + 0.26

   i 0.62 + 0.33   j 0.75 − 0.26   k 0.82 − 0.34   l 0.61 − 0.47

Challenge

Work out these calculations involving decimals with one, two or three places.

   a 0.5 + 0.263   b 0.15 + 0.631   c 0.8 + 0.742

   d 0.2 + 0.759   e 0.53 + 0.675   f 0.896 − 0.32

   g 0.745 − 0.3   h 0.886 − 0.1   i 0.9 − 0.634

   j 0.78 − 0.351   k 0.985 − 0.06   l 0.72 + 0.168

Calculations check-out

Practice

Write out the calculations, answer them and then choose a method of checking them.

	Calculation	Checking method
	4826 + 3941 = 8767	8767 − 4826 = 3941
a	25 + 17 + 39 + 29	
b	632 + 152	
c	7965 + 2391	
d	635 + 198	
e	8463 − 7963	
f	960 − 352	
g	14 + 25 + 36 + 98	
h	78 263 − 6354	
i	32 + 65 + 75 + 10	
j	963 + 472	
k	36 421 + 95 200	
l	63 + 35 + 14 + 37	
m	674 − 350	
n	7514 − 3000	
o	6800 − 2600	
p	8400 + 6100	
q	84 + 69	
r	6952 − 3841	
s	75 320 + 52 100	
t	9642 + 6300	
u	7500 − 2510	
v	82 + 63 + 41 + 37	
w	63 140 − 23 400	
x	8692 + 3471	
y	7210 − 6321	

Refresher

Work out the calculations and then check them using the suggested method.

1   Check these calculations by adding the numbers in the reverse order.

   a   31 + 25 + 51   b   74 + 38 + 20   c   61 + 53 + 87

   d   55 + 39 + 48   e   75 + 36 + 15   f   73 + 61 + 30

   g   12 + 36 + 59 + 84   h   32 + 52 + 16 + 62   i   13 + 20 + 46 + 53

   j   19 + 64 + 38 + 22   k   21 + 48 + 16 + 34   l   37 + 52 + 18 + 26

2   Check these calculations by using the odd and even rules.

   a   48 + 63   b   47 + 25   c   84 − 26

   d   40 − 27   e   486 − 201   f   255 + 320

   g   420 + 380   h   163 − 90   i   152 + 364

   j   271 + 632   k   286 − 42   l   437 + 193

3   Check these calculations by working out the inverse operation.
   You may use a calculator.

   a   4885 + 3621   b   8542 + 2704   c   7514 + 1397

   d   7852 + 5793   e   6985 + 3210   f   9862 − 3521

   g   5412 − 4213   h   4125 − 3781   i   6914 − 3823

   j   9621 − 3541   k   5861 − 4213   l   7061 − 3469

Challenge

Check these calculations to see if they are correct.
Write down the method you use.

   a   4536 + 8951 = 13 487   b   7861 − 3524 = 4347

   c   15 + 36 + 94 + 82 + 67 = 295   d   45 362 − 28 692 = 16 670

   e   23 855 + 14 869 = 38 624   f   6300 + 5800 + 9100 = 21 230

   g   78 330 + 78 251 = 156 581   h   89 + 62 + 37 + 15 + 96 = 299

   i   8563 + 6941 + 2871 = 18 365   j   48 362 − 25 032 = 73 394

Work it out!

Practice

Work out the answers to these problems.

1 Pitta bread is sold in packs of 6. The bags are packed in boxes.
  a If each box contains 30 packs. How many pitta breads does it hold?
  b If a supermarket has 4 boxes, how many packs do they have?
    How many pitta breads?
  c If a pack costs 63p, how much does a box cost?

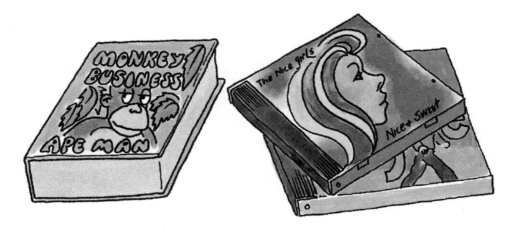

2 At the music shop a video costs £6·85 and a CD costs £9·45.
  a Jan bought a video and 2 CDs. How much did she spend?
  b Karen bought 2 videos and paid with a £20 note.
    How much change did she get?
  c A school buys 10 videos and 10 CDs. They get a 10% discount.
    What is their total bill?

3 A coach holds 52 passengers.
  a A school of 180 children and staff are going on an outing.
    How many coaches do they need?
  b Each coach costs £72 per day. How much will the school coaches cost?
  c The coach company has 12 coaches. If they are all full how many people
    will there be altogether?

4 A box of matches holds 98 matches. They come in packs of 10.
  a How many matches in a pack?
  b If I have 9800 matches, how many boxes do I have?
  c If I buy 100 packs, how many matches will I have?

Refresher

Work out the answers to these problems.

1 A tea cup holds 240 ml.

  a In a week Mrs Brown drinks 8400 ml of tea. How many cups is that?

  b The tea pot holds 2 l. How many full cups can be poured out of it?

  c If I drink 4 cups of tea a day, how much tea will I drink in a week?

2 Chocolate bars come in packs of 8.

  a The pack costs £1·84. How much is each bar?

  b I buy 10 packs. How much will that cost me?

  c 4 friends buy 1 pack and they each have 2 chocolate bars.
  How much does each friend pay?

Challenge

Think of 3 number problems. Work out the answers,
then give them to a friend to solve.

At the shoe shop I buy ...

1 bottle holds 450 ml ...

Think it through

Practice

Work out the problems. Explain how you worked out the answer to each question.

1 The decorator charges £18 an hour. Paint is £4·95 a tin.
   a He has given an estimate of £171·90. This includes two tins of paint. How long does he think the painting will take?
   b One week he earns £630 for his work. How many hours did he work?
   c To paint a whole house he estimates it will need 7 tins of paint and 26 hours work. How much will it cost?

2 The post person delivered 1800 letters today.
   a 30% of the letters were airmail letters. How many letters is this?
   b 5% of the letters needed signing for. How many letters is this?
   c 25% were postcards. How many is this?

3 Batteries come in packs of 2 or 4. A pack of 2 costs 95p, a pack of 4 costs £1·70.
   a Tim and Jack bought a pack of 4 and shared them. How much did they each pay?
   b Helen buys 2 packs of 2 and Mark buys 1 pack of 4. How much more does Helen pay?
   c Rebecca buys 10 packs of 4. How much does she spend?

4 a Julia buys 4 bags of crisps. She pays with a £2 coin and gets 60p change. How much is one bag of crisps?
   b Tom buys 10 bags of crisps. How much does it cost?
   c I have £1·75 to spend. How many bags of crisps can I buy?

Refresher

1 At the flower shop a bunch of tulips costs 99p and roses cost 50p each.

   a Lisa buys 4 bunches of tulips. How much does she spend?

   b John has £5 to spend on roses. How many can he buy?

   c Gavin buys 2 bunches of tulips and 2 roses. How much does he spend?

2 1480 people go to the school fair.

   a If everyone pays 60p to get in, how much was taken?

   b Coffee is sold for 40p a cup. 200 cups were sold.
     How much was spent on coffee?

   c 50% of the people that came were children.
     How many children came?

Challenge

Four girls are competing in the long jump. Sarah jumped 5 cm further than Louise and 8 cm further than Kate. Zoe jumped 10 cm further than Louise and 4 cm further than her best friend, Rachel.

If Kate jumped 252 cm, how far did the other girls jump?

Odds and evens

Practice

Use the numbers shown to complete these sentences.

Remember

Remember to try at least five examples before making a general statement.

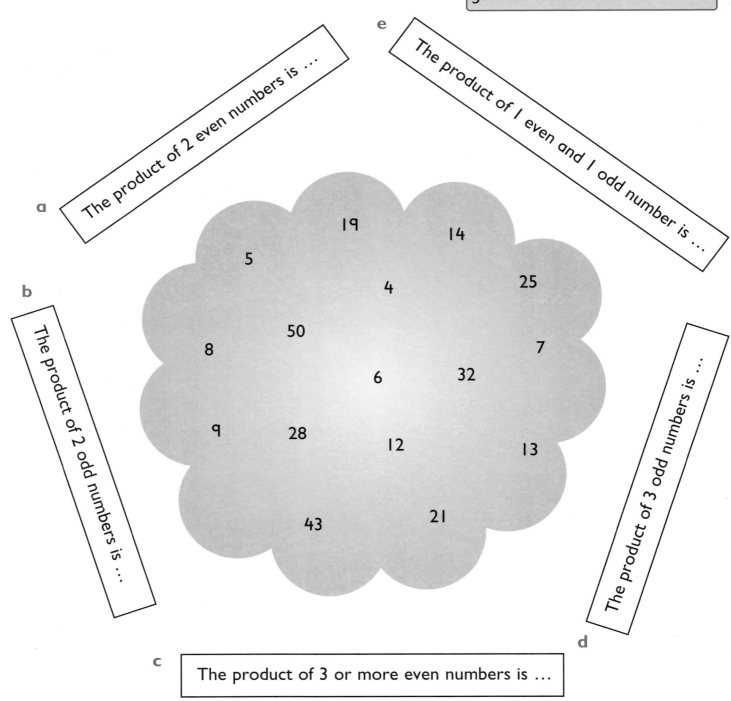

a **The product of 2 even numbers is ...**

e **The product of 1 even and 1 odd number is ...**

b **The product of 2 odd numbers is ...**

d **The product of 3 odd numbers is ...**

c **The product of 3 or more even numbers is ...**

Numbers: 19   14   5   4   25   50   8   7   6   32   9   28   12   13   43   21

Refresher

1 Use these statements about odd and even numbers to help you decide whether the answers to the calculations below could be correct.

2 Write the calculations that could be correct.

a 18 + 22 = 50   b 26 + 88 = 104   c 45 + 33 = 77

d 27 + 79 = 106   e 12 + 14 + 16 = 44   f 52 − 34 = 38

g 89 − 47 = 51   h 47 + 65 = 112   i 15 + 27 + 39 = 72

j 123 + 259 = 382   k 86 + 92 = 179   l 76 − 44 = 32

m 97 − 63 = 35   n 128 + 146 = 276   o 77 + 114 = 182

p 73 + 48 = 112   q 243 − 137 = 106   r 36 + 47 = 83

s 181 − 97 = 84   t 326 − 140 = 186   u 152 − 36 = 123

v 271 + 273 = 445   w 235 + 262 = 498   x 94 − 76 = 11

3 Using the calculations you have written, check to see if the answers are correct.

Remember

The sum of 2 or more even numbers is even.

The sum of 2 odd numbers is even.

The sum of 3 odd numbers is odd.

The sum of an odd number and an even number is odd.

The difference between 2 even numbers is even.

Challenge

Some of the calculations are incorrect.

1 Use the statements in the Refresher section, and the statements you made about finding the product of odd and even numbers, to determine which calculations could be correct.

2 Write the calculations that could be correct.

3 Work out the answers to check if they are correct.

a 686 − 498 = 188   b 24 × 15 = 370   c 3476 + 4598 = 8374

d 76 × 8 = 618   e 8 × 12 × 14 = 1345   f 3257 − 1243 = 2037

g 7 × 9 × 11 = 693   h 6 × 12 × 24 = 1748   i 39 × 17 = 763

j 638 + 422 + 374 = 1435 k 47 × 51 = 2398   l 85 × 25 = 2125

m 364 + 228 + 126 = 694 n 84 × 19 = 1586   o 163 × 7 = 1141

p 298 × 8 = 2287   q 93 × 27 = 2510   r 59 × 42 = 2473

s 74 × 36 = 2664   t 14 × 8 × 24 = 2635   u 13 × 5 × 9 = 587

Find the common multiples

Multiples which are the same for 2 or more numbers are called **common multiples** of those numbers.

Example

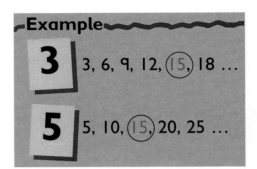

3 | 3, 6, 9, 12, (15,) 18 …

5 | 5, 10, (15,) 20, 25 …

1 Write the first 10 multiples for each pair of numbers. Circle the common multiples for each pair.

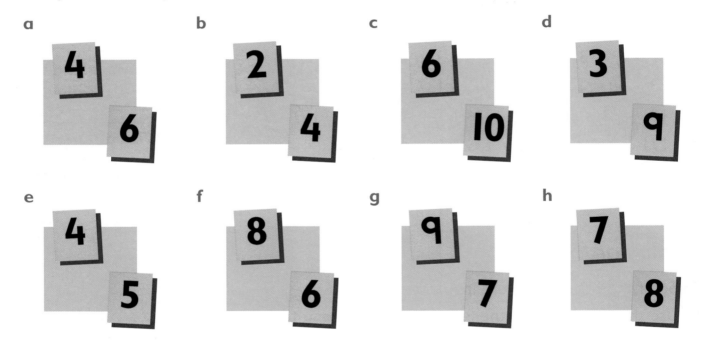

a

4
6

b

2
4

c

6
10

d

3
9

e

4
5

f

8
6

g

9
7

h

7
8

2 Write the first 10 multiples for each set of 3 numbers. Circle the lowest common multiple.

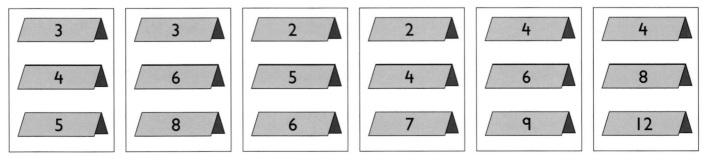

3	3	2	2	4	4
4	6	5	4	6	8
5	8	6	7	9	12

3 If there are no common multiples in any of the sets above, work out what number would be the lowest common multiple.

Refresher

1 a The numbers have escaped! Find the multiples of 4, 6 and 9.
b Write a multiplication fact for each multiple you find.

Challenge

Try these problems.

1 a Make a list showing multiples of 8 and 15.
b Find 4 common multiples.
c What is the lowest common multiple?

4 What is the fourth common multiple of 12, 15 and 20?

2 John and Peter begin football practice today. John practises every 3 days and Peter practises every 5 days. How many days until they practise together again?

3 a Write the first 5 multiples of 99.
b What pattern do you notice?
c Continue the pattern. What happens?

5 A green light flashes every 24 seconds. A red light flashes every 36 seconds. If they start at the same time, how often do they flash together?

Divisibility tests

Practice

1 a Write the first 10 multiples of 25.
   b What do you notice about the multiples of 25?
   c Copy and complete the rule for the multiples of 25.

> The multiples of 25 ....
>
> ....

2 Write a divisibility rule for 25.

> A number is divisible by 25 if ....
>
> ....

3 Find the numbers that are divisible by 25.

> 2050   1625   1710   3475   6770   23 250
> 9000   47 125   25 235   33 475   6700   25 320

4 Which of these numbers are divisible by 0·25?

> 3·25   5·00
>   7·50
> 7·45   3·75
>   2·10
>   6·20
> 4·65   9·25

5 A number is divisible by 4 if the last 2 digits divide exactly by 4.
   Find the numbers that are divisible by 4. Show your working.

6 A number is divisible by 8 if half of it is divisible by 4 or its last 3 digits are divisible by 8
   Find the numbers that are divisible by 8. Show your working.

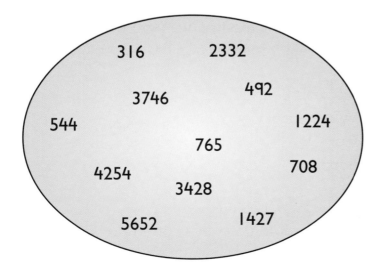

316   2332
      492
3746
544   1224
      765
4254   708
   3428
5652   1427

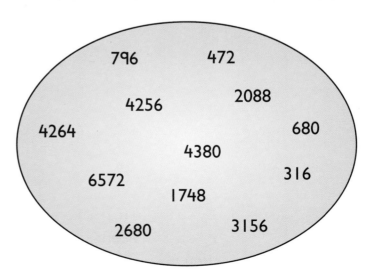

796   472
            2088
4256
4264   680
      4380
6572   316
      1748
2680   3156

Refresher

Copy and complete the next 5 numbers in these number sequences.

a 0·25, 0·50, 0·75, 1·00, _____, _____, _____, _____, _____

b 4, 8, 12, 16, _____, _____, _____, _____, _____

c 8, 16, 24, 32, _____, _____, _____, _____, _____

d 6·50, 6·75, 7·00, 7·25, _____, _____, _____, _____, _____

e 10·00, 9·75, 9·50, _____, _____, _____, _____, _____

f − 64, − 56, − 48, _____, _____, _____, _____, _____

g 16, 12, 8, 4, _____, _____, _____, _____, _____

h 2·50, 2·25, 2·00, _____, _____, _____, _____, _____

Challenge

Use your knowledge of the divisibility tests to answer these problems.

a 25 pictures a second are transmitted to television sets. This means that in 3 minutes 4500 pictures are transmitted. Could this be true? How do you know?

b Leap years occur every 4 years. Will the year 2068 be a leap year? How do you know?

c Write all of the leap years that will occur this century.

d An octagon has 8 sides. Is it possible to make complete octagons using 768 sides? How do you know?

e There are 4 gills in a pint. Could full pints be made using 2596 gills? How do you know?

f The Highlands in Scotland is populated by just 8 people per square kilometre. Could the total population be 3504? How do you know?

Divisibility testing time

Practice

A number is divisible by:

2 if it is an even number and the last digit is 0, 2, 4, 6 or 8

3 if the sum of its digits is divisible by 3

4 if the tens and units digits divide exactly by 4

5 if the last digit is 0 or 5

6 if it is even and it is also divisible by 3

8 if half of it is divisible by 4 or if its last three digits are divisible by 8

9 if the sum of its digits are divisible by 9

10 if the last digit is 0

1 The boxes below have lost their labels. Use the divisibility tests to find which set of multiples are in each box and write a new label.

2 One number does not belong. Write it down.

3 Explain how you worked out which numbers belong in each set.

a
4262   3750
    2756
1364   4323
    3196
3782   6148

Multiples of ...

b
4638   8397
    3420
2393   3870
    2718
7527   6804

Multiples of ...

c
4800   1872
    3120
2688   3984
    1920
3074   4652

Multiples of ...

d
3432   4792
    3520
1388   2264
    4312
1912   2176

Multiples of ...

e
1296   3132
    3528
1512   1944
    2483
2808   3060

Multiples of ...

f
4320   1602
    5610
3243   2625
    2931
7428   3735

Multiples of ...

4 Use the tests of divisibility to write 5 numbers:

   a divisible by 3 between 400 and 500
   c divisible by 5 between 2000 and 2500
   e divisible by 9 between 4000 and 6000

   b divisible by 4 between 600 and 2000
   d divisible by 6 between 700 and 1500
   f divisible by 8 between 200 and 800

Refresher

Write the answers to these problems.

a 10 even numbers between 500 and 1000.

b 10 multiples of 5 between 200 and 500.

c The multiples of 4 up to 100.

d The multiples of 3 up to 60.

e Five 3-digit numbers where the sum of the digits adds up to 9.

f Five 3-digit numbers where the sum of the digits adds up to 18.

g 10 3-digit numbers where the sum of the digits is divisible by 3.

Challenge

Use your knowledge of divisibility tests to help you devise divisibility tests for other numbers.

Show examples of numbers that do not fit your test also, to show that your test works.

11

- Write a list of multiples of 11.
- Devise a test of divisibility for 11.
- Try your test out on larger numbers. Use a calculator to check if your test works.

12

- Use the fact that $3 \times 4 = 12$ to develop a test for divisibility by 12.
- Try your test out on larger numbers. Use a calculator to check if your test works.

103

Prime numbers

Practice

 Remember

● A prime number is a number that has only 2 factors, itself and 1.
● A composite number has more than 2 factors.
● 1 is neither a prime nor a composite number.

This table shows the numbers from 1 to 6 with their factors.
It also shows the total number of factors each number has.

Number	Factors	Number of factors
1	1	1
2	1, 2	2
3	1, 3	2
4	1, 2, 4	3
5	1, 5	2
6	1, 2, 3, 6	4

1 Draw your own table like this. Find the factors for all the numbers up to 50. Use your table to answer these questions.

2 Make a list of all the numbers you found with only 2 factors.
What are these numbers called?

3 Make a list of all of the numbers you found that have 3 factors.
What are these numbers called?

4 What sort of numbers have an odd number of factors?
Explain why.

5 Can you predict any numbers up to 100 that might have
a 3 factors
b an odd number of factors
c How did you work this out?

Refresher

Draw and continue each factor tree to find
the prime factors of each of these numbers.

Example

16

4 × 4

2 × 2   2 × 2

2 is the only prime factor

a

36

4 × ☐

b

48

6 × ☐

c

40

4 × ☐

d

24

3 × ☐

e

72

9 × ☐

f

96

6 × ☐

g

100

4 × ☐

Challenge

Try these:

1 Are square numbers prime or
composite? Explain your reasons.

2 The sum of the digits in the number 14
are prime, for example, 1 + 4 = 5. Can
you find 10 other numbers like this?

3 17 is a prime number. Reverse the
digits. Is the new number prime?
Find other pairs of numbers like this.

4 a Which of these numbers could
not be a prime number:
502, 299, 392, 1795, 462
b Explain your reasons.

5 Are there fewer prime numbers
or composite numbers? Explain
your reasons.

Glossary

angles

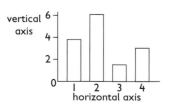

right angle

acute angle

obtuse angle

180° straight line

Angles are formed when two straight lines meet. We measure an **angle** by measuring the amount of turn from one line to the other.

Angles are measured in degrees. The symbol for degrees is °.

A right angle is 90 degrees, 90°. A right angle is shown by a small square.

An acute angle is less than 90°.

An obtuse angle is more than 90°.

A straight line has an angle of 180°. This can be used to work out the second angle.

arc

Any part of the circumference of a circle is called an **arc**.

See also circumference

area

Area is the amount of surface of a shape. It is measured in square centimetres. This can be abbreviated to cm^2.

You can work out the **area** of a rectangle by multiplying the length of the shape by the breadth. Length × breadth = **area**.

average

The **average** is the middle amount in any range of data.

You calculate the average by adding all the amounts then dividing by the number of items.

Marks in a maths test		
Joe	42	Average = 42 + 55 + 67 + 59 = 224
Sue	55	224 ÷ 4 = 56
Helen	67	The average score is 56
Sam	59	

Mean is another word for **average**.

axis, axes

vertical axis

horizontal axis

Graphs and charts have two **axes**.

The horizontal **axis** shows the range of data.
The vertical **axis** shows the frequency. They can be labelled in any equal divisions.

brackets	**Brackets** are used in maths for grouping parts of calculations together.

brackets

Brackets are used in maths for grouping parts of calculations together.

$10 - (3 + 4) = 3$

$(10 - 3) + 4 = 11$

The calculations in brackets need to be worked out first.

capacity

Capacity is the *amount* that something will hold.
Capacity is measured in litres and millilitres.
1 litre is equal to 1000 millilitres.

Litre can be abbreviated to l.
Millilitres can be abbreviated to ml.

Capacity can also be measured in pints and gallons.

See imperial units

circumference

The **circumference** is the distance all the way round a circle.

column addition

When you add large numbers, using the standard vertical method can make the calculation easier.

The numbers must be written with the digits of the same place value underneath each other.

If the digits in one column add up to more than 9, the tens are carried to the next column.

column subtraction

Th	H	T	U
⁴5̷	¹7	¹2̷	5
− 3	8	0	6
1	9	1	9

When you subtract large numbers, using the standard vertical method can make the calculation easier.

The numbers must be written with the digits of the same place value underneath each other.

◀ If the top digit is lower than the bottom digit then 10 can be "borrowed" from the next column.

common denominator

A **common denominator** is when two or more fractions have the same denominator.

Fractions with different denominators need to be changed to have a **common denominator** before they can be added or subtracted.

$\frac{1}{2} + \frac{1}{4}$ can be changed to $\frac{2}{4} + \frac{1}{4}$

The **common denominator** is 4.

See also equivalent fraction

concentric

Concentric means *with the same centre.*

These circles are **concentric**.

co-ordinates

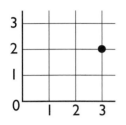

Co-ordinates are numbers or letters that help us to plot the exact position of something. We use them on maps, graphs or charts.

◀ Graphs like this are called the first quadrant.

On the graph, the dot is at (3, 2) 3 lines across and 2 lines up.

To read **co-ordinates** we look *across* and *up*. Some people remember this by thinking of "Along the corridor, up the stairs".

decimals

Decimal fractions show us the part of a number that is not a whole number.

The decimal point separates the whole numbers from the decimal fractions.

H	T	U	●	ths	hdths
		5	●	8	
		5	●	8	6

◀ Each digit after the decimal point has a different place value.

5·8 is a number with one decimal place.
5·86 is a number with two decimal places.

Decimals and fractions

All decimals have a fraction equivalent. To find the decimal equivalent for a fraction we divide 1 by the denominator and then multiply by the numerator.

$\frac{3}{4}$ = 0·75

1 ÷ **4** = 0·25

0·25 × **3** = 0·75

$\frac{1}{2}$ = 0·5

$\frac{1}{4}$ = 0·25

$\frac{3}{4}$ = 0·75

$\frac{1}{10}$ = 0·1

$\frac{3}{10}$ = 0·3

$\frac{1}{5}$ = 0·2

$\frac{1}{100}$ = 0·01

$\frac{3}{100}$ = 0·03

See also fractions

divisibility

There are some quick tests you can do to see if one number will divide by another.

You can use your knowledge of multiplication facts: $3 \times 4 = 12$ so 12 is divisible by 3 and 4.

Other tests:

2s   Any even number is divisible by 2.

4s   If you can divide the last two digits of the number by 4 exactly, the whole number will divide exactly by 4. 216 is divisible by 4 as 16 is divisible by 4.

5s   You can divide 5 exactly into any number ending in 5 or 0.

10s   If a number ends in 0 you can divide it by 10 exactly.

100s   If a number ends in two zeros it will divide exactly by 100.

1000s Any number that ends in three zeros is divisible by 1000.

dividing by 10, 100 and 1000

When a number is **divided by 10, 100 or 1000** the digits move one, two or three place values to the right. If the hundreds, tens and units digit is zero it disappears, if it is not zero it becomes a decimal.

The place value of the digits decreases 10, 100 or 1000 times.

See also multiplying by 10, 100 and 1000

dodecahedron

A **dodecahedron** is a solid shape with 12 faces.
The faces are pentagons.

equivalent fractions

Equivalent fractions are fractions of equal value. They are worth the same.

$\frac{4}{8}$ is equivalent to $\frac{1}{2}$

See also common denominator

See also fractions

factor

A **factor** is a whole number which will divide exactly into another whole number.

The factors of 12 are 1, 2, 3, 4, 6, 12 as they all divide into 12.

The factors can be put into pairs. If the pairs are multiplied together they will equal 12.

1 × 12
2 × 6
3 × 4

formula

A **formula** is a way of writing down a rule.

For example, to find the area of a rectangle you multiply the length by the width.

fractions

Fractions are parts of something.

$\dfrac{1}{2}$ → numerator
→ denominator

The numerator tells you how many parts we are talking about.
The denominator tells you how many parts the whole has been split into.

fractions and division

We find fractions of amounts by dividing by the denominator and then multiplying by the numerator.

We divide by the denominator as this is the number of parts the amount needs to be divided into. We then multiply by the numerator as this is the number of parts we are talking about.

See also fractions

imperial units

These used to be the standard measurements in Britain. They have now been replaced by metric units. Some imperial units are still used today.

Capacity
1 pint = 0·568 l
8 pints = 1 gallon

Length
1 yard = 0·914 m
1 mile = 1·6 km
1 inch = 2·54 cm
1 foot = 0·305 m

Mass
1 ounce (oz) = 28·35 g
1 pound (lb) = 16 ounces

improper fraction

An **improper fraction** is a fraction where the numerator is more than the denominator.

$\frac{13}{5}$

These are sometimes called top heavy fractions.
Improper fractions can be changed to whole numbers or mixed numbers.

◄ $\frac{5}{4} = 1\frac{1}{4}$

◄ $\frac{8}{4} = 2$

A fraction that is not an **improper fraction** is a proper fraction.

See also fractions
See also mixed numbers

integer

Integer is another name for a whole number.

See also whole number

intersection

If two lines **intersect** they cross each other.

These lines intersect at **A**.
A is the point of intersection.

inverse operations

Inverse means *the opposite operation*. The **inverse operation** will undo the first operation.

Addition and subtraction are **inverse operations**:
17 + 26 = 43   43 − 26 = 17

Multiplication and division are **inverse operations**:
6 × 9 = 54   54 ÷ 9 = 6

length

Length is how long an object or a distance is.
Length is measured in kilometres, metres, centimetres and millimetres.

1 kilometre is equal to 1000 metres.
1 metre is equal to 100 centimetres.
1 centimetre is equal to 10 millimetres.

Kilometre can be abbreviated to km.
Metre can be abbreviated to m.
Centimetre can be abbreviated to cm.
Millimetre can be abbreviated to mm.

Length can also be measured in miles.

See also imperial units

| **long division** | When you divide numbers which are too large to work out mentally, you can use **long division**. We call it **long division** when both numbers involved are two digits or more. |

long multiplication

		3	5	2
×			2	7
	7	0	4	0
	2	4	6	4
	9	5	0	4
			1	

When you multiply numbers which are too large to work out mentally, you can use **long multiplication**. We call it **long multiplication** when both numbers involved are more than a single-digit.

The numbers must be written with the digits of the same place value underneath each other.

See also short multiplication

mass

Mass is another word for weight.
Mass is measured in grams and kilograms.
1 kilogram is equal to 1000 grams.
Mass can be measured in pounds and ounces.

See also imperial units

mean

Mean is another word for average.

See also average

median

The **median** of a range of data is the item that comes *halfway*.

Marks in a maths test
46   51   52   (60)   62   65   71
60 is the **median**.

mode

The **mode** of a set of data is the number that occurs most often.

multiplication

Multiplication is the inverse operation to division.
Numbers can be multiplied in any order and the answer will be the same.
$5 \times 9 = 45$ $9 \times 5 = 45$

See also inverse operations

multiplying by 10, 100 and 1000

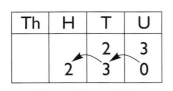

Our number system is based around 10.
When a number is **multiplied by 10, 100 or 1000** the digits move one, two or three place values to the left and zeros go in the empty column to keep its place value.

◄ The place value of the digits increases 10, 100 or 1000 times.

See also dividing by 10, 100 and 1000

$23 \times 10 = 230$

multiples

A **multiple** is a number that can be divided into another number.

2, 4, 6, 8, 10, 12 are all **multiples** of 2 as we can divide 2 into them all.

10, 20, 30, 40, 50, 60, 70 are all **multiples** of 10 as we can divide 10 into them all.

Multiples can be recognised by using the multiplication facts.

negative numbers

Numbers and integers can be positive or **negative**.
Negative integers or numbers are *below* zero.

Negative numbers have a minus sign before them.
–56

Negative numbers are ordered in the same way as positive numbers except they run from right to left.

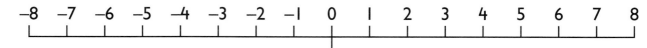

net

A **net** is a flat shape which can be cut out and folded up to make a solid shape.

<, >, ≤, ≥

are symbols used to order numbers.

< means less than   45<73
> means more than   73>45
≤ means less than or equal to   45≤45, 46
≥ means more than or equal to   87≥87, 86

ordering fractions

When you **order fractions** and mixed numbers, first look at the whole numbers then the fractions. If the fractions have different denominators, think about the fractions in relation to a half to help you to order them.

parallel

Parallel lines are lines that are the same distance apart all the way along.

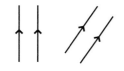

◀ They are often shown by two little arrows.

parallelogram   A **parallelogram** is a four-sided shape with its opposite sides parallel to each other.

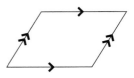

percentage   The sign % stands for *per cent*, which means out of 100.
30% means 30 out of 100.

Percentages are linked to fractions and decimals.
$\frac{1}{2}$ = 50% = 0·5
$\frac{1}{4}$ = 25% = 0·25
$\frac{3}{4}$ = 75% = 0·75
$\frac{1}{5}$ = 20% = 0·2
$\frac{1}{10}$ = 10% = 0·1

Finding percentages of amounts

To find **percentages** of amounts we need to use the relationship to fractions.

To find 50% of an amount, we divide by 2: 50% = $\frac{1}{2}$.
50% of £40 is £20.

To find 25% we divide by 4: 25% = $\frac{1}{4}$
To find 20% we divide by 5: 20% = $\frac{1}{5}$

perpendicular   A **perpendicular** line meets another line at right angles.

perimeter   **Perimeter** is the distance all the way around a flat shape.

You can calculate the **perimeter** of a shape by adding the length of all the sides together.

If a shape has sides all the same length then you can use multiplication to work out the **perimeter**.

4cm
3cm
3 + 4 + 3 + 4 = 14cm

pie chart   A **pie chart** is a way of showing information

Y6 journeys to school

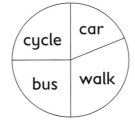

plane A **plane** is a flat surface.

prime factor A **prime factor** is a factor which is also a prime number.

See also prime number

See also factor

prime number **Prime numbers** are numbers that can only be divided by 1 and themselves.

A prime number has only two factors.

17 is a prime number. It can only be divided exactly by 1 and 17.

1 is not counted as a prime number.

The prime numbers to 20 are:

2, 3, 5, 7, 11, 13, 17, 19

probability **Probability** is about how *likely* or *unlikely* the outcome of an event is. The event may be the throw of a die or whether or not it will rain today.

We use certain words to discuss **probability**. We can put events and the words on a scale from *no chance of it happening* to *certain*.

| impossible no chance | unlikely | even chance | possibly likely | good chance | certain |

Even chance means an event is as likely to happen as not happen.

product **Product** is another name for the answer to a multiplication calculation.

24 is the product of 6×4

proportion **Proportion** shows the relationship between two connected things.

When amounts are being compared and they have equal ratios they are in **proportion**.

1 packet of biscuits costs 60p
2 packets of biscuits cost £1·20
3 packets cost £1·80
The cost is in **proportion** to the number of packets bought.

See also ratio

quadrant

A **quadrant** is a quarter of a circle.

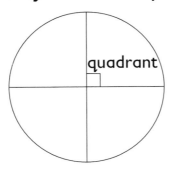

Quadrants are used in graphs.

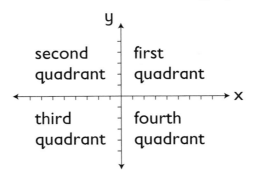

quotient

Quotient is another name for the answer to a division calculation.

The remainder of the **quotient** can be shown as a fraction or a decimal fraction.

$27 \div 4 = 6 \text{ r } 3$

$27 \div 4 = 6\frac{3}{4}$

$27 \div 4 = 6 \cdot 75$

As we are dividing by 4, the fraction will be a quarter and there are 3 of them left. $0 \cdot 75$ is the decimal equivalent to $\frac{3}{4}$.

range

The **range** of a set of data is the lowest to the highest value.

ratio

Ratio is a way of comparing amounts or numbers.

It can be used in two ways:

It can describe the relationship between *part to whole*.
A cake is divided into 4 equal parts and one part is eaten. The **ratio** of part to whole is one part in every four parts or 1 in 4.

Or it can describe the relationship of *part to other part*.
A cake is divided into 4 parts and one part is eaten. The ratio of part to part is 1 to 3 as for every piece eaten three pieces are left.

The **ratio** 1 to 3 can also be written as 1:3.

See also proportion

reflection

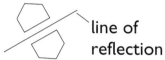
line of reflection

◀ If a shape is **reflected**, it is drawn as it would appear reflected in a mirror held against or alongside one of its sides.

reflective symmetry

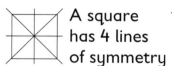
A square has 4 lines of symmetry

A shape is symmetrical if both sides are the same when a line is drawn through the shape. The line can be called a mirror line or an axes.

◀ Some shapes have more than one line of symmetry.

rhombus

A **rhombus** is a four-sided shape.
Its sides are all equal in length.
The opposite sides are parallel.

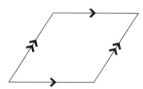

round number

A **round number** usually ends in a zero. When using or estimating with large numbers round numbers are easier to work with.

short division

When you divide numbers that are too large to work out mentally, you can use **short division**. We call it **short division** when one of the numbers involved is a single-digit.

short multiplication

When you multiply numbers that are too large to work mentally, you can use **short multiplication**. We call it **short multiplication** when one of the numbers involved is a single-digit.

◀ The numbers must be written with the digits of the same place value underneath each other.

See also long multiplication

square numbers

To **square** a number it is multiplied by itself. The answer is a **square number**.

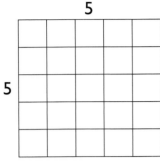

To square 5, we multiply 5 by itself. 25 is the **square number**.

◄ $5 \times 5 = 25$ can also be written as $5^2 = 25$

Square numbers have an odd number of factors. The factors of 25 are 1, 5, 25.

Square numbers up to 100

$1 \times 1 = 1$
$2 \times 2 = 4$
$3 \times 3 = 9$
$4 \times 4 = 16$
$5 \times 5 = 25$
$6 \times 6 = 36$
$7 \times 7 = 49$
$8 \times 8 = 64$
$9 \times 9 = 81$
$10 \times 10 = 100$

See *also* factor

symmetrical pattern

Patterns can be **symmetrical**. They may have two lines of symmetry.

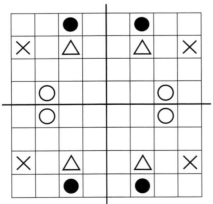

line of symmetry

line of symmetry

time

These are the units **time** is measured in:
seconds
minutes
hours
days
weeks
months
years

These are the relationships between these units:
60 seconds = 1 minute
60 minutes = 1 hour
24 hours = 1 day
7 days = 1 week
4 weeks = 1 month
12 months = 1 year
365 days = 1 year

analogue   digital
clock   clock

◄ **Time** can be read on analogue clocks or digital clocks.

Digital clocks can be 12 hour or 24 hour.
The 12-hour clock uses a.m. and p.m.
The 24-hour clock carries on after 12 o'clock midday to 24 instead of starting at 1 again.

translation

A **translation** is when a shape is moved by sliding it.

trapezium

A **trapezium** is a four sided shape with two parallel sides.

triangles

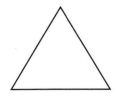

A **triangle** is a 2D shape with three straight sides and three angles.

There are four kinds of triangle:

Equilateral triangle
◀ This has three equal sides and three equal angles.

Isosceles triangle
◀ This has two equal sides. The angles opposite these two sides are also equal.

Scalene triangle
◀ All three sides are different lengths.
The angles are all different too.

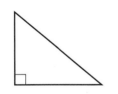

Right-angled triangle
◀ This has one right angle.

vertex

The **vertex** is the tip or top of a shape, the point furthest away from the base. The plural is **vertices**.

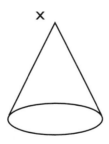

x is the **vertex** of the cone

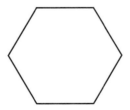

A regular hexagon has 6 vertices

120